A Primer for
SPIRITUALITY
in the 21st Century

ROBERT C. WILD

A Primer for SPIRITUALITY in the 21st Century
Copyright © 2019 by Robert C. Wild

All rights reserved. No part of this publication may be reproduced, distributed, or transmitted in any form or by any means, including photocopying, recording, or other electronic or mechanical methods, without the prior written permission of the author, except in the case of brief quotations embodied in critical reviews and certain other non-commercial uses permitted by copyright law.

Tellwell Talent
www.tellwell.ca

ISBN
978-0-2288-1606-5 (Paperback)

FRONTISPIECE

Languages are mortal,
like plant and animal species,
and like species
they displace one another
as their territories shift.
If it is going to survive,
a language, like a species,
needs a habitat and an ecological niche.

Robert Bringhurst
Everywhere Being Is Dancing

Perhaps the most challenging of all the ingredients of feminist spirituality is the naming of God, a naming that points to the mystery of divinity beyond any name.

Mary T. Malone
Women and Christianity, Vol 3.

TABLE OF CONTENTS

1. The Cosmic Sacred 1
2. The Hebrew Exception 8
3. Story-Telling 14
4. History And Mythology 24
5. Prophecy In Ancient Israel 35
6. Four Gospels: Text In Context 41
7. Apocalytic Eschatology 59
8. Jesus' Alternative Spirituality 69
9. The Apostle Paul 75
10. Realm Of The Sacred 81
11. Aboriginal Wisdom 92
12. Gospel, Law And Admonition 98
13. Ego, Soul And Spiritual Life 103
14. The Journey 115
15. Creating A Pilgrim's Notebook 122

End Note On Depth Psychology 125
Select Bibliography 127
About Bob Wild 131

INTRODUCTION

During the late 19th and early 20th centuries, ancient scrolls from the earliest Jesus Movement were discovered in regions around the Dead Sea. These items prompted scholarly re-assessment of the earliest Christian communities: their historical context, teaching, and legacy. These documents - together with previously-discovered 5th century scrolls of the New Testament - prompted better translations of that text and a wide-ranging debate about the nature of Christian origins.

This debate did not change my convictions about the centrality of Jesus of Nazareth for the meaning of human existence, but it challenged me to share with others some consequences of these important academic discussions.

In 2004 I published my book "Sacred Presence: in Search of the New Story". In that book I replaced use of the word 'God' by 'Sacred Presence'. The traditional word God is strongly associated with 'out there'; I used 'Sacred Presence' to bring attention to the dynamic of Spirit within the entire Created Order. Increasingly I have felt the need to recognize and emphasize the immanence of the Sacred within planet Earth as the foundation of everything. In this book I seek to identify the roots and expression of a spirituality which can respond to this Presence of the Sacred.

Robert Wild
Salt Spring Island, BC, Canada
2019

1

THE COSMIC SACRED

There is a crisis in religious faith in the West revealed in a widespread disconnect from traditional Christian symbolism and practice. Though our hearts may yearn for spiritual truth, a great many people find that the symbolism of contemporary religion does not speak to their need. For centuries the Christian religion has been anchored in symbolism using power language like Eternal Father, Lord, King, Majesty, Saviour, the Almighty, and Salvation or Damnation. As an anchor for religious faith, this language is for many people now inadequate, or irrelevant, or simply obsolete. This symbolism seems to belong to ages clearly removed from our own. Thoughtful people are drifting away from the churches because most of the familiar metaphors for the Sacred no longer seem to carry social power or intellectual integrity.

On the other hand, there is a general reawakening of interest in spiritual aspects of human nature. We are aware that there is more to us than our physical senses and appetites and intellectual achievements. Many of us want to develop a functional understanding of, and creative expression for, our personal spiritual yearning. How can we find some continuity between the long history of religious expression in the West and our own questions and searching?

We know that the universe in which we live came into existence about 14 billion years ago from a cataclysmic eruption of unimaginable force which scientists call the Big Bang. After more than 10 billion years of universe building, during which matter and space were being created in a rapid and enormous dispersion of energy, a tiny planet emerged from an exploding star. This star is our Sun, this planet is our Earth.

The continuing, long evolution of the material order resulted eventually in the emergence of life. Late in life's diversification and increasing complexity, it became expressed in the genus *mammal* within which the species *homo* emerged. Perhaps 150,000 years ago the subspecies *homo sapiens sapiens* began its evolution into what human nature is today. And about 30,000 years ago primitive hunter-gatherer societies evolved with spiritual awareness which allowed an elusive communion between humanity and a felt Sacred Presence.

AWE, FEAR and MORTALITY

With the evolution of human self-consciousness, our earliest ancestors developed an intuitive response to the power and beauty and abundant resources of the natural world. They were awestruck. And in response to the chaotic, unpredictable and often destructive events of wind and water, fire and storm, they experienced a nebulous fear.

Self-consciousness continued to develop. The inevitability of death caused humans to imagine delectable places beyond present existence on Earth: happy hunting grounds where loved ones would continue their life journeys. More recently, the continuing experiences and speculations of humans led to a variety of sophisticated belief systems which postulated spiritual realms holding mysterious sacred powers. Having no rational explanation for the powerful forces of Nature, they imagined supernatural realities - both benevolent and malevolent - which controlled the world. Feelings of awe, fear and hope for a future life were a few of the building blocks of an enriching self-consciousness.

Within this long process in humans of a developing awareness of the Sacred Other, there emerged a generalized psychic activity of *imaginative projection*. Psychic projection allows humans to sense 'spirit' within an array of objects in the surrounding world. In some societies every significant element in Nature had its spirit aspect. For some people their psychic powers of projection discerned 'manna' (blessing) as a unique quality of the Sacred Others. In still other societies projection took the form of designating certain birds, animals and fish as tribal 'totems', supernatural beings who were seen as integrated with the life of the group. And for us today, as we consider this wide variety of early imaginings, it is difficult to draw firm lines of separation between magic, religion, and rational curiosity. These three seem to have developed together very early in human self-consciousness and only later to have evolved into separate and distinct social attitudes and practices.

PRIMITIVE RELIGION

A supernatural, sacred world 'existed' for early peoples because something in the human heart profoundly desired this to be true. No measurable evidence was required in these societies to validate the existence and actions of the Sacred. What was being experienced and expressed mythologically came to have profound social and personal significance. *The Sacred 'existed' as co-respondent to the felt spiritual yearnings and aspirations of people.* Each aspect of early religious devotion and practice derived its meaning and power through a creative relationship with the Sacred Others who 'existed' through the agency of unconscious human projection.

Rituals emerged everywhere to guide and govern human response to these mysterious realms of the Sacred. By ritual acts humanity expressed its relationship to those mysterious Others, to a Sacred Realm beyond direct human sensual experience. Communal acts of adoration, supplication and propitiation provided appropriate means by which humans avoided feeling totally vulnerable to these imponderable, supernatural forces. And, concurrent with this development, there appeared a class of revered men and women who acted as a bridge between the human and the Sacred: witches and witch doctors, shamans and sorcerers, priests and priestesses.

FORMAL RELIGIOUS PRACTICE

The development of agriculture allowed roving hunter-gatherer family groups to develop settled, communal village life. Clusters of villages evolved into towns and cities with more complex patterns of social organization. As different classes of people emerged to become overseers of the several segments of city life, the practice of religion became centred in the persons and responsibilities of a priestly class. Religious feelings, convictions and practices became organized into elaborately practiced ceremonies. Formal religion became managed by priestly hierarchies.

Sociological studies describe the composition of higher agricultural societies as similar in shape to a drop of water waiting to fall: a very narrow neck at the top and widening out to a large bulge. The small neck points to 9% of the total population, representing monarchy, aristocracy, the military, priesthood and merchants. A poor and oppressed peasantry formed the large remainder. In these societies, the divine Subjects of religious practice gradually shifted from aspects of Nature to supernatural human beings. Rituals exalted these divinized human figures; these rituals ensured that the populace would provide the necessary tributes to sustain local cults.

In Near-Eastern religions, the Gods were the source of both blessing and judgment. The Gods were adored, propitiated and supplicated in order to secure their blessing. And when blessings in social or personal life seemed to be absent, the Gods were presumed to be displeased. In such circumstances, the priesthood prescribed what the people must do by way of propitiation of the deities, to make positive the deities' relationships with the community. This religious activity resulted in enormous prestige and social power being vested in the priesthood.

At present, within our appreciation of this historical evolution of religion, we can also recognize both the roots and strength of a contemporary religious skepticism and the continuing 'hunger' in human nature for secure spiritual roots.

HUMAN SPIRITUALITY AND THE SACRED

Spiritual awareness is recognized today as a significant element in the evolution of human nature. Our consciousness had its antecedents in earlier mammalian life; our self-consciousness represents a definitive stage in human spiritual development. 'Spirituality' is a recently popular term to name the interior processes or energies which mark us as *homo sapiens sapiens*. We know that we are more than we feel and think as earthlings. We wonder who we are, where our being came from, and where it is going.

Our ability imaginatively to project our human feelings and aspirations upon and into other life forms led to the symbolism of both magic and religion. Spiritual impulses present in human nature caused us to seek for spiritual co-respondents in the world around us. Humanity populated the heavens with a multitude of gods; formal religious practices became expressed in language, drama, plastic arts and music. As sketched above, this process represents a long development in human efforts to find creative expression and nourishment for spiritual yearnings. Moreover, there is no indication today that we can do entirely without some kind of creative religious self-expression through appropriate symbol systems. Imaginative, creative symbols and metaphors are essential both for our mental and spiritual health and as a means of opening ourselves to the Sacred.

It may sometimes seem to us today that the proliferation of deities throughout the millennia of human societies represents only the results of imaginative projection, of 'reification' - the materialization of what is imagined. On the contrary, depth psychology has demonstrated that we have active psychic resources which are independent of our volition and imagination and which function without our conscious participation. Our sense of the Sacred can have a true objectivity (i.e. not be simply a result of subjective projection) because each human psyche is open to both the personal and the collective Unconscious. Within our deep psychic structures are functions which open us to the Mystery of the Sacred according its own Reality. Lives of people in many cultures provide us with clear examples of this potential and of its creative results. As with these people of former times, stories in our contemporary personal experience reveal the presence of the Sacred within and around us.

JESUS OF NAZARETH IN CONTEXT

The recent century and a half of scholarly research into the significance of biblical texts supplies us with new perspectives on Jesus of history as a faithful Jewish man living within a specific time and place. That time and place was the country of Palestine then subject to imperial Rome, of an ancient People restless and rebellious under occupation by a rapacious foreign power. Jesus' response to that world has startled and challenged countless people for over 2000 years.

In this book I reflect on the historical Jesus as manifesting in himself both a profound response to the age-old spiritual yearnings of human beings, and as a unique revelation of the Loving, Yearning and Grieving Sacred Presence who transcends time and place.

As we learn to give careful attention to our deepest personal desires, and as we explore this experience using imagination and creativity, we may find new depths of meaning and spiritual nourishment offered to humanity in this Man of Galilee.

Questions for discussion:

1. What elements in Christianity do you now find encouraging or enlightening? perplexing or unacceptable?
2. Where do you place yourself now within a secularist / religionist continuum?
3. What factors are moving you at present towards either position?

2

THE HEBREW EXCEPTION

It is not known precisely how and when a nomadic/pastoral people, later to be known as 'Hebrews', came to reside in what is today northern Palestine. The archaeological evidence is scant and many of the stories about their earliest years have no clear, historical veracity. Nevertheless, the full complement of their biblical narratives holds significance, both then and now, for their self-understanding as the People of Yahweh.

The ancient Hebrews developed a unique approach to their historical experience through a process of remembering, rehearsing, recording and reflecting on their stories. Prof. Bernhard Anderson ("Out of the Depths") makes this important observation about ancient Israel:

> The pre-eminent context in which to understand the Hebrew Scriptures is in their responses to their remembered experiences as a people.

The wealth, power and regional importance of the ancient Hebrews reached their highest point during the 8th century BCE. Ten northern tribes - known as Israel or Ephraim - occupied the most fertile parts of the land of the ancient Hebrews. Their capital city of Samaria greatly outshone in wealth and power the relatively small and unimportant town of Jerusalem, central for two southern tribes known as Judea. To the East lay the empire of the Assyrians with ambitions to occupy and possess the affluent territory of Israel. In the year 722 BCE, Samaria fell to overpowering Assyrian armies and the ten northern tribes of Israel disappeared into the expanding empire.

The enduring significance of this disaster for the future of the Hebrew People was in the desperate flight of the élite of the ten northern tribes to the southern city of Jerusalem. Temple priests and scribes of the northern tribes took with them oral traditions and sacred writings which told stories about their relationship with their God, Yahweh. Key segments of these northern written traditions are found scattered in the first five books of the Bible and have been designated by modern scholars as 'E' (for Ephraim). Later in the same century, in the city of Jerusalem, this written material from the north was blended with complementary written material already existing in Judea. Some of this southern material, known today as 'J' (also found scattered in the first five books of the Bible), was blended with 'E'. It is identified now as JE. Also preserved to accompany JE were well-developed oral traditions providing verbal commentary on the written word. A thoroughly re-edited version of these founding narratives was also produced at this time in Jerusalem, known to us as the biblical document Deuteronomy.

It is important to realize that these early writings were 'history mythologized'. Stories about the originating patriarchs - Abraham, Isaac and Jacob - were knit together with stories about Moses and Joshua. Some of this blended material became an 'escape narrative' which remembers the ancient Hebrews' release from slavery in Egypt; some became the story of the occupation of the 'land of the Canaanites'. The total complex of these many stories became a sacred mythology which provided late 8th century Hebrews with vital self-understanding. By means of this newly-shaped national narrative they understood themselves to be the chosen People of Yahweh.

Notice the difference between this process used by the Hebrews to evolve their national religious traditions and the process used by other Near Eastern peoples to identify the sacred beings of their respective pantheons. The Canaanites, Assyrians, Egyptians, Persians, Romans, Greeks and others developed *their differing sacred mythologies concerning their several gods by the process of collective psychic projection*. Each cultural group established its respective Sacred Realm as focused around specific divine persons and rituals. Each society imaginatively established the content of a specific religion for their own people. The Hebrews, in contrast, developed their spiritual traditions by *imaginative reconstruction of their collective, national memory*. Yahweh became the One God who as an objective Sacred Presence was believed to take the initiative in real historical time to shape and continually reshape the destiny of his chosen People.

Here are two small sections of the biblical text which illustrate central aspects of the Hebrew view of their God. The first is a Mosaic commandment:

> You shall not make to yourself a graven image, or any likeness of anything that is in the heaven above, or that is in the earth beneath, or that is in the water under the earth; you shall not bow down to them or serve them; for I the Lord your God am a jealous God... (Ex 20:4-5)

The second section is from the ritual of Covenant Renewal between Yahweh and his people, used annually during certain periods of their history. In these verses, the national leader Joshua is pictured as speaking to the tribes of Israel gathered at Shechem:

> Thus says the God of Israel... I took your father Abraham from beyond the River and led him through all the land of Canaan, and made his offspring many. I gave him Isaac; and to Isaac I gave Jacob and Esau... I sent Moses and Aaron, and I plagued Egypt... I brought you to the land of the Amorites... I gave them into your hand... I gave you a land on which you had not laboured... (Josh 24:1-13)

The categorical prohibition against representing the divine Presence in any material form (Exodus 20) is complementary to the proclamation by Yahweh as being himself the primary active agent in their national history: 'I took, I gave, I sent, I brought, I plagued'. *Yahweh is believed to act and to be discernible within history,* though He is not a tangible Presence. The Hebrews found their basis for spiritual communion with the Divine through a Sacred Presence whom they believed guided their national history.

Development of symbolic language about Yahweh took place over many centuries, taking the form of an increasingly complex trajectory of images. The earliest image may have been of Yahweh as the **Compassionate God** who suffered with his People who were in the bondage of slavery in Egypt: 'I have seen my People and I will deliver them from the yoke of slavery'. Closely associated with that image is the **Warrior God** who fought with the Israelite army to occupy the lands of the Canaanites. In the first seven books of the Bible, Yahweh is pictured as mobilizing and leading armies of the Israelites against their enemies.

As the Hebrews developed permanent settlements, Yahweh also became pictured as Israel's **Lawgiver and Judge**. Ten Commandments became the core text of an extensive body of Law which emerged to provide regulations for both domestic life and temple worship. This legal corpus implied both creative divine judgment and the punishment of wrongdoers. Still later Yahweh was pictured as One who **enters into Covenant** with his people.

The relationship with Yahweh God now had an explicit element of reciprocity: 'If you obey my commands I will bless you, but whenever you disobey my commands I will punish you.' Gradually, over several centuries, this evolving tradition of images became interwoven into a tapestry of faith and practice which reminded Israel of the Sacred Presence in whom the nation was grounded.

There is an additional image, however, which does not share the same kind of historical roots. In company with her neighbours, Israel developed stories about the 'early times': fables about the Garden of Eden, of Cain and Abel, and of the great Flood. In the 7th century BCE, when Israel's cultural leaders were in Exile in Babylon, they conceived and composed the poetic narrative of Genesis Chapter One. Here Yahweh precedes the nation's Story as the **Creator** who exists outside the historical process which was being fashioned as Israel's emerging national narrative.

This five-fold imagery concerning Yahweh became central to the continually developing sacred text of the Hebrew Scriptures. And, judging by the documents of the New Testament, the first disciples of Jesus of Nazareth accepted this five-fold image of Yahweh, with a significant emphasis on 'compassion'. This is the religious context within which the historic Christian Church based her teaching about Jesus of Nazareth.

Questions for discussion:

1. To what extent is this Hebrew teaching about Yahweh relevant today in light of our present understanding of Earth and the Cosmos?
2. Using a Bible, read Gen 15:1. This may be the oldest verse in the formation of the Hebrew Scriptures. What elements of this text indicate its time of origin? Why is it correct to understand this as mythology and not as history?
3. Compare Gen 12:1-9 with 17:1-8. What elements of each 'call story' made these passages important for the early formation of the Hebrew tradition?
4. Tell a story of an important personal life experience which you can recall vividly. Which elements of this story are history and which are mythological?

3

STORY-TELLING

For most of the last 2000 years the Bible has been referred to by the Christian Church as the 'Word of God'. Taken literally, to name the Bible in this way is misleading if not downright wrong - though this way of speaking is valid as a metaphor. Even though God doesn't have a mouth, and human ears are designed only to hear certain physical wave motions present in the air, when reading the Bible a great many people have attested to 'being addressed' by a Sacred Presence, by a sacred Word.

To find a more adequate way of approaching the Bible I suggest that we frame a different metaphor, focused in a question: *What do we learn from the Hebrew and Christian Scriptures about the possibility and the nature of encounter between the human and the Sacred?*

CORE SACRED STORIES

Here and there in the Hebrew and Christian Scriptures we find what I propose to name as 'core sacred stories'. These were *remembered events* which named and sought to illuminate the mystery of Divine/human encounter. These events were recorded for the instruction of future generations. These stories are 'sacred' because each attempts to describe a mystical encounter *the meaning of which cannot be described adequately by using only the common data of life in time and space.* Each such story uses the subtle arts of mythological expression to quicken our imagination, to challenge our understanding, and to encourage us to open our own lives to the leading of the Spirit. These are 'core' stories because each one, together with associated 'satellite' texts, point to the heart of the biblical message. In some manner or other each story seeks to express the mystery of divine Presence and Power as this has engaged the story-teller.

When reading biblical literature we must keep in mind that 'every text has a context'. We must ask about each text: who remembered and recorded it? when? where? and for what reason? I am always disappointed (and disconcerted) when in church liturgies biblical readings are given without any introduction, as though context is not important. It is all-important.

Here is an example of a core sacred story. A Hebrew man known to us as Isaiah of Jerusalem (c.BCE 750-690) reported a Divine/human encounter which he experienced in the Jerusalem temple. He uses language typical of such stories.

> In the year that King Uzziah died I saw the Lord sitting upon a throne, high and lifted up; and his train filled the temple. Above him stood the seraphim; each had six wings: with two he covered his face, and with two he covered his feet, and with two he flew. And one called to another and said:
>
> "Holy, holy, holy is the Lord of hosts; the whole earth is full of his glory."
>
> And the foundations of the thresholds shook at the voice of him who called, and the house was filled with smoke. And I said: "Woe is me! for my eyes have seen the King, the Lord of hosts!"

> Then flew one of the seraphim to me, having in his hand a burning coal which he had taken with tongs from the altar. And he touched my mouth, and said: "Behold, this has touched your lips; your guilt is taken away, and your sin forgiven." And I heard the voice of the Lord saying, "Whom shall I send, and who will go for us?" Then I said, "Here I am! Send me."
> (Isa 6:1-8)

Isaiah was gripped in one sacred moment by an overwhelming sense of the Presence. From the records of his many subsequent oracles in the Book of the Prophet Isaiah, we know that he was profoundly troubled by the immoral social life and hypocritical religious practice of Judah. Through his encounter with the Presence he was vividly reminded of these social ills and of his own complicity in them. But in spite of this complicity he was being chosen and sent to the people to be a vessel of Yahweh's Word of warning, and for their possible spiritual healing.

Isaiah was one of those persons who can be described as *radically open to the Divine.* Persons who are taken into this kind of mystical encounter are usually deeply sensitive to the moral and religious failures in their own lives and in their communities. During the encounter event, the customary 'felt distance' between the human and the Divine is momentarily overcome. This 'felt distance' between them arises from two qualitative separations: a separation in Being - the Divine from the human, and a separation in moral character - absolute Goodness from moral equivocation. In mystical encounters this 'double distance' is momentarily overcome by a divine initiative which directly engages the consciousness of the human person in order to bring insight, healing and new responsibility. *But the meaning of this kind of experience can only be described in symbolic terms.* Each event is a mysterious, unique and sublime occasion of soul-making; each needs and uses the symbolic language and imagery of mystery in order for it to be shared with others.

Reports of such encounters are not limited to the Hebrew Scriptures but are found in every religion. Such encounters can also come as a result of a strange human awareness of the Sacred in Nature. Innumerable inventions of word, music, dance and the plastic arts have been created to suggest what occurred in the encounter, and to share the meanings experienced. But the personal feelings of what occurred cannot be reproduced as originally experienced. Though rich, extensive and creative symbolism is employed, these testimonies can only try to suggest the significance of mystical experience within the human soul. And since the ancient Hebrews had an unusual capacity for storytelling, it was the medium of words which they used chiefly to relate spiritual consequences of encounter with the Presence.

THE CYCLE OF JACOB STORIES

Chapters 27 to 33 of the book Genesis provide a long and dramatic account of decisions and actions taken by central participants in the formative centuries of the ancient Hebrews (probably earlier than 900 BCE). This one, long Story seeks to reveal how Yahweh accomplished his loving purposes for his people *through human experiences, decisions and actions present in many separate encounters with the Holy One.*

It is impossible to tell how much detail in these stories is historically accurate and how much is a storyteller's invention. But the end result is a beautiful account of Yahweh weaving together the good and the bad in the hearts and deeds of these people in order to achieve the purposes of the Holy One. Even the unworthy and deceitful machinations of Rebekah, Jacob, Laban and Rachel enable sacred purposes to be realized. (I recommend the entire Cycle for a good read.)

The biblical redactors use the extensive dialogue and dramatic actions of their characters to show how each person fulfills Yahweh's intention. The ultimate goal of this repeated divine guidance is to have the patriarch Jacob beget twelve sons, the men who will later head the twelve tribes of 'Israel' - Jacob's new name. On two occasions Jacob is directly involved in personal encounter with the Presence, and both are core stories of Divine/human encounter within the full cycle of stories.

> Jacob came to a certain place, and stayed there that night, because the sun had set. Taking one of the stones of the place, he put it under his head and lay down in that place to sleep. And he dreamed that there was a ladder set up on the earth, and the top of it reached to heaven; and behold, the angels of God were ascending and descending on it! And behold, the Lord stood above it and said, "I am the Lord, the God of Abraham your father and the God of Isaac; the land on which you lie I will give to you and your descendants... and by you and your descendants shall all the families of the earth bless themselves. (Gen 28:11-16)

Jacob sent his close family members across the ford of Jabbok and he was left alone. A man wrestled with him until the breaking of the day.

> When the man saw that he did not prevail against Jacob, he touched the hollow of his thigh; and Jacob's thigh was put out of joint as he wrestled with him. Then he said, "Let me go, for the day is breaking." But Jacob said, "I will not let you go, unless you bless me." And he said to him, "What is your name?" And he said, "Jacob". Then he said, "Your name shall no more be called Jacob but Israel, for you have striven

with God and with men, and have prevailed." Then Jacob asked him, "Tell me, I pray, your name." But he said, "Why is it that you ask my name?" And there he blessed him. So Jacob called the name of the place Peniel, saying, "For I have seen God face to face, and yet my life is preserved."
(Gen 32:24-30)

Commentators on the stories of the Jacob Cycle praise their high literary quality, which is astonishing considering their age (these two core stories about Jacob may be nearly 3000 years old). This is sacred story telling at its best. If you read the entire Cycle perhaps you will feel the power which this has had for countless generations of Jacob's people, and understand how their faith in Yahweh was constantly renewed as they entered into the stories.

ARCHETYPAL STORIES

The creativity of the Bible's core sacred stories derives in part from their nature as 'archetypal'. That is: they illuminate *characteristic moments of humanity's ongoing spiritual journey*, and they point to profound depths of human spiritual life. When we listen to these stories with active imagination and spiritual hunger they have power to assist experiences of Divine/human encounter in our own lives. From this point of view, there are at least three trans-historical questions embedded in the archetypal structure of the second Jacob story given above: How shall I name the Sacred? What is the nature of my own struggle with the Sacred? Do I have a personal name which signifies to me the essence of who I am?

During these very early times in Israel's history, before they began to develop a written tradition, their community memory of core sacred stories was in the custody of a group of well-trained storytellers. It was their responsibility to remember and retell their people's stories; they were the custodians of a unique oral tradition.

Some of the best known stories are those which concern Abraham (Gen 12:1-3 and 17:1-21), Jacob (Gen 27-33), Moses (Ex 3), a large Semitic slave group in Egypt (Ex 15:1-12), Hannah (1 Sam 1), Samuel (1 Sam 3), and David (1 Sam 17).

Anthropologists' knowledge of the work of both traditional and contemporary storytellers assures us that this process of oral transmission had a well-developed and dependable form. Designated story-tellers faithfully repeated what they were commissioned by the community to remember.

SCRIBES IN ANCIENT ISRAEL

To the southwest of the newly-emerging Hebrew People (c.1000-850 BCE), in the more ancient civilization of Egypt, there was already a well-developed class of literate scribes whose work was to record the public affairs of their people. Anthropologists have demonstrated that this Egyptian scribal tradition influenced the development of similar skills in Israel. But we don't know whether Egyptian scribes were brought to the court of Israel's monarchy to be trainers of Israelite men as scribes, or whether Israelite men were sent to the Egyptian court to be taught the new skill there.

It was this increasingly important class of Israelite scribes who over several centuries put into writing the oral traditions of their community's core sacred stories and embellished them with satellite material. Some of this satellite material was already in the community memory; other texts were composed in the scribal schools. In this manner many different kinds of document were both shaped by, and helped to give shape to, Israel's sacred texts: laws (for the regulation of ritual, social and personal life), prophetic oracles, historical narrative, devotional poetry, and wisdom literature. The resulting collection eventually came to be known as the Hebrew Scriptures.

It was in this ancient Hebrew tradition that Jesus of Nazareth found his social and spiritual roots. And these Scriptures, and the community they shaped, provided the immediate context and background within which documents of the early Jesus Movement were conceived and written after his death.

STORY TELLING TODAY

In recent decades many people have been encouraged to develop an interest in writing about and reflecting upon their life stories. Courses of instruction for keeping a daily journal have become popular and manuals of instruction are available for this purpose. A very old art is being rediscovered and revalued.

In taking up this practice we may discover that some of our personal stories are rooted in experiences of the beauty and wisdom of the natural environment. Earth is our home. Our stories are also profoundly conditioned by family life, how we earn our daily bread, by the quality of our relationships with other people, and by the turbulence and uncertainties of the contemporary world scene. In our storytelling, as in biblical times, context shapes text. And in the midst of all this inner/outer dialogue, personal encounters with the Sacred can appear, unexpected and arresting. Here are two stories of this kind of experience, one from Christian tradition and one from my journal.

ABOUT FRANCIS OF ASSISI

Francis was riding listlessly in some wayward place, apparently in the open country, when he saw a figure coming along the road towards him and halted; for he saw it was a leper. And he knew instantly that his courage was challenged, not as the world challenges, but as one would challenge who knew the secrets of the heart of a man... Francis Bernadone saw his fear coming up the road towards him, the fear that comes from within and not without; though it stood white and terrible in the sunlight. For once in the long rush of his life his soul must have stood still. Then he sprang from his horse, knowing nothing between stillness and swiftness, and rushed on the leper and threw his arms round him. It was the beginning of a long vocation of ministry among many lepers for whom he did many services. To this man he gave what money he could and mounted and rode on.

(G.K. Chesterton, *Francis of Assisi*)

FROM MY PERSONAL JOURNAL

During an overseas walking pilgrimage in 1980, I visited for several days in the Lake District of northwest England. From there I traveled south on Lake Windermere to Bowness, planning to walk from there overland to the town of Kendal. I found the correct footpath but, as I walked, it gradually disappeared into an open field. A friendly farmer directed me to the roadway and suggested I walk there instead.

The June morning was cool, overcast and drizzling. My backpack was heavy and some body joints and muscles were complaining. The day was turning out to be miserable. By late afternoon I arrived at the upper end of a long and gentle slope leading into the town of Kendal. As I walked disconsolately down the slope I noticed a tiny figure in the distance coming towards me. Gradually the figure developed into a person and then, closer, into a plump country woman carrying a loaded shopping basket. When she was close to me she stopped and said, "'Tis a fine day for a hike!" I stopped, surprised, and she continued, "May the road rise to meet you, may the wind be always at your back. May the sun shine strong upon your face, and the rain fall softly on your fields. And may God hold you in the hollow of his Hand." Then she reached over, put her hand on mine, and with the brightest of blue eyes looking steadily into my own she said softly, "And may the Lord bless you." Then she was gone. I have not before nor since felt more blessed. A dismal day was transformed with light.

Question for discussion:

> Consider whether you remember and treasure 'core sacred stories' in your own lifetime which, if retold now, might prove helpful to other people.

READING AND REFLECTING ON THE BOOK OF PSALMS

The Book of Psalms has been a staple in Christian liturgy from the 2nd century Desert Fathers until the present. The poetry is frequently beautiful; the aspirations for righteous living can be inspiring. Many of these texts incorporate the traditional images of Yahweh (Powerful Creator, Eternal Lawgiver, Punisher of offenders, Defender of his Chosen People). New readers can easily become discouraged by these particulars of a culture now embedded far back in history. On the other hand, some of the Book of Psalms is worth reading and reflection today. Here are the numbers of some psalms useful for personal consideration and reflection, always remembering that their context is the world of the Near East in the 1st millennium BCE:

4, 16, 19, 22, 23, 29, 31, 32, 34, 36, 40, 46, 51, 57, 62, 65, 84, 85, 91, 95, 96, 102, 103, 111, 119:73-88, 97-112, 121, 127, 130, 139; 1-18, 23-24, 145, 146.

Each psalm witnesses to one or more of the five characteristic ways in which Yahweh was believed to be present to his people. As you read, notice how the poetry expresses one or more parts of this faith tradition.

4

HISTORY AND MYTHOLOGY

myth - uses a dramatic person or event, real or imagined, to reveal meaning in human existence

mythology - is community elaboration and social expression of myths

History is an attempt to record for posterity the course and endeavours of human life on this planet. We might be tempted to think that history deals with indisputable, objective facts. However, deeper reflection reveals that historical writing is always tempered by the insights, biases and values of those who record it. The personal and social contexts of each observer/recorder are reflected in their historical writing. As the popular saying has it: "There is no truth about the past - there are versions only."

In contrast to historical writing - which attempts to minimize value judgments - mythology intentionally describes and elaborates value-laden myths. Mythology responds to implicit questions about human origins, meaning and destiny by employing the media available: story-telling, poetry, music, pictorial arts, dance, film, architecture, etc. Mythology is not primarily concerned with rationality and logic, though it does not intentionally violate common sense. To be relevant, mythology must be consistent with contemporary understanding of the material cosmos and of the current social mores.

A healthy culture develops its own myths and mythology which blend with the integrated spiritual traditions to offer meaning and moral guidance for social and personal living. Spiritual tradition and mythology seek to offer a workable context within which members of a given society can understand themselves and their world and find guidance for their daily living.

Mythology makes use of the free range of imagination as it moves between reflecting ordinary sensory world realities and engaging in extremes of fantasy. But it wasn't until the seminal work of Sigmund Freud and Carl Jung, beginning over a century ago, that our imaginative mythological endeavours were revealed as profoundly shaped and coloured by the human unconscious, both personal and collective. The creativity of the human unconscious knows no bounds and mythology is one of its most fruitful endeavours.

The Hebrew Scriptures provide interesting examples of the mutually supportive mix of history and mythology, of history mythologized. Biblical scholars today attempt to describe the cultural context of a given text so as to help readers to be aware of the special circumstances and specific community interests which created that text's final form. And in addition to the critical factor of social context, archaeology has often been able to provide significant external, physical data which might challenge the presumed historical veracity of certain biblical texts. There is more creative mythology in the Bible than believers have usually acknowledged.

ISRAEL'S GRAND NARRATIVE

Ancient Israel's biblical narrative begins with a cycle of early stories about the patriarchal period. In the Book Genesis we read about Abraham, Isaac and Jacob, and of Jacob's twelve sons. We are told that this important family group started life in the city of Ur of the Chaldees and gradually moved about until they eventually settled in Egypt. These narratives are followed in the Book Exodus by stories of deliverance from slavery in Egypt and of desert wanderings. During this time Moses is pictured as receiving their sacred Law from Yahweh God. Finally, to close the Grand Narrative there are conquest and settlement stories in the Books of Joshua, Judges and Samuel which tell how the Israelites occupied the territory of the Canaanites and became consolidated into twelve tribes.

If we read these ancient stories with the question, 'What actually happened?' we become thoroughly confused. For example, the several lists (and partial lists) of the Twelve Tribes of Israel (understood to be descendants of the twelve sons of Jacob) are not consistent with one another. Moreover, the authors' several descriptions and evaluations of the significance of each tribe reveal wide discrepancies. Nor is it always possible to create a chronology of these biblical records which is consistent with limited external data available from neighbouring peoples.

Scholars have known for over a century that the several differing themes in these books represent different vested interests within the emerging people of Israel. Documents which are represented as historically accurate are actually the products of diverse special interest groups. Biblical writings reflect the complex dynamics within an emerging nation trying to understand and elaborate its own story. Moreover, a key problem for understanding this material has been the scarcity of external data which could accurately provide us with the biblical people's place in the ancient Near East. Only within recent decades has a satisfactory framework been provided by new archaeological finds in the land of Palestine.

MYTHOLOGY RATHER THAN HISTORY

During the 10th and 9th centuries BCE the people we know as ancient Israel gradually took possession of lands occupied by the more ancient Canaanite people of today's land of Palestine. By about 1000 BCE they had formed themselves into twelve tribes. The ten northern tribes (known as Israel) had the best agricultural land, and their capital city Samaria acquired considerable wealth and power. But to the east the nation of Assyria had become an imperial power with designs to overrun and occupy all neighbouring peoples, including Israel. By the year 722 this purpose had been accomplished through military conquest of the ten northern tribes and by their assimilation into the empire of Assyria. They ceased to exist as a distinct people.

In their book, "The Bible Unearthed" (2001), biblical scholar Israel Finkelstein and archaeologist Neil Asher Silberman provide the necessary framework for understanding the dramatic consequences for Israel of these 8th century events for the ensuing life of the ancient Hebrews. Within their discussion of the foundational documents of ancient Israel they make this observation concerning traditional biblical stories about the monarchies of David and Solomon (p.144):

> These were theological hopes, not accurate historical portraits. These [theological hopes] were a central element in a powerful seventh century vision of national renaissance that sought to bring the scattered, war weary people together, to prove to them that they had experienced a stirring history under the direct intervention of God. The glorious epic of the united monarchy [of David and Solomon] was - like the stories of the patriarchs and the sagas of the Exodus and conquest - a brilliant composition that wove together ancient heroic tales and legends into a coherent and

persuasive prophecy for the people of Israel in the seventh century BCE.

Though there is no detailed information in the biblical text about how the court in Samaria reacted to the Assyrian threat, Finkelstein and Silberman use definitive archaeological data linked to the biblical narrative to propose a probable sequence of events during the late eighth century BCE. These data invite us to imagine a gradual exodus of refugees fleeing to the southern territory of the two remaining Israelite tribes, of which Jerusalem was the main centre. When these two ethnically related groups became blended into one, this "scattered, war weary people" *discovered an urgent need to provide themselves with a common sacred story.* The leaders of both Israel and Judah, now working together, produced "a brilliant composition that wove together ancient heroic tales and legends into a coherent and persuasive prophecy". Though some of those editors may have thought they were recording history, in fact *they were creating a national mythology based in traditional stories.* They used a creative and imaginative method, expressed in a very sophisticated capacity for descriptive language, to conjure for themselves their significance as one people living together under one divine Being.

And buried in this extensive and creative mythology lies the answer to the most fascinating question of all: *What spiritual experiences caused the leaders of these newly-united peoples to discover ethical monotheism as the key to their national history and purpose?* The eventual result of that long process became revealed in the five-fold Naming of Yahweh.

AN EXPANDING MYTHOLOGY

As noted above, late in the eighth century imperial Assyria overcame the northern Israelite peoples by invasion and assimilation. During succeeding decades Assyria also harassed the Judahite towns in the south, especially the capital city Jerusalem. But this threat ceased abruptly when another imperial power, Egypt, came from the southwest to reclaim Judah as a subject territory. And then, later still, this national overlord was replaced by a more powerful imperial force from the east. Early in the seventh century, armies of the rising power Babylon (also known as Chaldea) swept into Judah. They destroyed the temple in Jerusalem and took all the leading persons of Judah into exile in the eastern city of Babylon. Subsequent chronicles of exiled Israel interpreted these traumatic events within their newly-elaborated mythology:

> And the Lord sent against [Judah's King, Jehoiakim] bands of the Chaldeans, and bands of the Syrians, bands of the Moabites, and bands of the Ammonites, and sent them against Judah to destroy it, according to the word of the Lord which he spoke by his servants the prophets. Surely this came upon Judah at the command of the Lord, to remove them out of his sight, for the sins of Manasseh [a recent king of Judah], according to all he had done, and also for the innocent blood that he had shed; for he filled Jerusalem with innocent blood, and the Lord would not pardon. (2 Kings 24:2-4)

The Hebrew exiles in Babylon (perhaps a few thousand people, BCE 589) accepted their changed circumstances without excessive rancour and proceeded to reorganize their common life. Not having the temple in Jerusalem as the centre of community life and faith, they now saw themselves as 'People of the Book'. Using memories and documents from earlier times, they extended the Sacred Story in which they were portrayed as Yahweh's chosen people. A national history/ mythology was extended and revised to include their new situation in Exile. Scholars speak of this ongoing expansion and re-editing of tradition as 'the work of redaction'. This is a well-recognized literary process by which an existing written tradition becomes revised and renewed in line with new social circumstances.

The priestly establishment had lost their formerly prominent position as custodians of the sanctuary and its ceremonies. Now, by careful redactional working of their sacred texts, including a record of life during the Exile, the priesthood ensured that they would have a continuing vital role and authority within the believing community.

Elements of their redactional work can be seen in textual material designated by scholars as the priestly document (P). This is found in several places in the first five books of the Bible but chiefly in the Book Leviticus, and notably in the first chapter of Genesis. This enchanting poem of the foundational work of Yahweh has for centuries provided a great many believers with a sacred Story of the Creating God. However, because its dated mythological character is obvious, this powerful Story has no obvious place in the reconstruction of faith today.

A FUNCTIONAL MYTHOLOGY

Wherever it occurs, a strong mythological tradition expresses a spiritual essence of the society which both creates it and is created by it. *There is a dynamic interplay between what is being created and the people who do the creating.* The two grow in tandem, a dialectical unity.

If we recall and reflect on personal life stories - yours or mine - we find that the most vivid events are those which provide insights into the person each of us is in our daily becoming. And our stories-as-remembered always stretch beyond 'the facts' to include colourful details by which we hope to name, remember and reveal some of the inner significance of our life. By our storytelling we renew and enrich ourselves and one another. Personal experience needs and creates mythological vehicles in which to be expressed.

We continue to read the Bible for the same reason. Dramatic stories of a spiritual tradition not only carry value-laden memories of the past, they have power to elicit similar meanings and values in the present. Good stories are opaque: they invite creative questions and imaginative response in the hearers. Good stories are multivalent: they are capable of influencing people in different ways.

The enduring 'questions about God' in the Bible have received many responses over the centuries. Nevertheless, as I have already suggested, there were five key images of Yahweh which emerged and remained central in the evolution of Hebrew and Christian faith. The ancient Hebrew divinity, Yahweh, was first imaged as a *Warrior* god who was an echo of older Canaanite deities. He was believed to fight with Israel's armies. Later, Yahweh was imaged as the divine *Lawgiver and Judge*. His Will was heard and announced; his punishment was proclaimed against Israelites who disobeyed him. A modification of this image emerged later as Israel discovered a *covenant relationship* with their God. Though He would punish their disobedience, He would give blessings to those who obey. The fourth image was of the *Creator* God. A fifth and muted image of a *compassionate* God is visible in the prophets and in a few of the psalms. This latter image is the one which Jesus of Nazareth made central in his own teaching and public actions.

Biblical Israel never left out any of these images of her God and all five continue to exist in the Hebrew Scriptures in contrast and complementarity. This creative conflation of images was inherited and adopted by the new Jesus Movement as it shaped the emerging orthodox Christian doctrine of God - but *without due attention to modifications which were implicit in Jesus' teaching*. For example: wherever Christian nations have claimed God's blessing for their armies in battle we can observe the very old Warrior god being invoked. Or again, many church-goers have been so well instructed in the Ten Commandments that the divine Lawgiver's punishment is anticipated by many of the faithful when they disobey. Christian orthodoxy, sadly, has yet to recognize that the image of a Compassionate Sacred Presence supersedes or modifies all other four images of the Sacred.

MYTHOLOGIES ARE BORN AND DIE

Myths and mythology have always been important in the human adventure because humans continually seek meaning for life and we picture that meaning in imaginative ways. Each person becomes unconsciously conditioned by the mythology of her or his own social group, with its particular slant on the meaning of human life. And existing myths and mythology eventually die as new myths and mythology are born to replace them.

Hebrew/Christian mythology became central to European imagination and social conditioning during the 1st millennium CE. The Christ Myth pictures four dynamic 'moments' in its Story: Creation, Fall, Redemption, and Eternal Salvation. In the first chapter of my book, *Sacred Presence: in Search of the New Story*, I argued that during recent centuries this Christ Myth gradually became obsolete among us as we responded to another mythology. This mythology was born in response to the expanding wisdom of the natural sciences, and to a surge of new information and material techniques. It has given birth to the powerful mythology of 'technological progress'.

This mythology is becoming increasingly dominant on planet Earth wherever industrialization occurs. Many Western people have in practice left behind the Christ Myth and its supernatural mythology and have been won over to the attractive and persuasive mythology of technological society and its material rewards.

Very recently, however, the cutting edge of the mythology of technological progress has been dulled by a growing public awareness of threats to the natural environment resulting from the daily operations of our highly industrialized society. For many people, Rachel Carson's book of 1963, *Silent Spring*, was a wake-up call. For others, the alarm is being sounded in the continuing devastation of land and forests, of sea and air, and through climate change. It is still uncertain whether humanity can halt the depredations of the technologically-committed corporate world order in time to secure the survival of Earth's integrity.

IN SEARCH OF NEW MYTHS AND MYTHOLOGY

As a result of the uncertain status of much social and cultural life in our present world, many people are now left without a convincing Story by which to be inspired and guided. *We are a society which has no widely accepted and empowering spiritual vision and commitment.* On the other hand, already there are small signs of the birth of a new mythology (representing a new spirituality?) which is Earth-centred. "The earth is not a collection of objects, it is a communion of subjects", suggests eco-theologian Thomas Berry. Several sciences demonstrate that everything in the cosmos is interrelated; Aboriginal spiritual traditions are reviving their own witness to the sacredness of Earth.

One basic challenge to the Christian Church today is to recognize Earth as a Revelation of the Sacred. There is a fundamental unity between human spirituality and Mother Earth. Earth and Spirit are not antagonistic: each yields its own testimony to the Sacred. We need a contemporary mythology to express this unity.

HISTORY, MYTHOLOGY AND SPIRITUALITY

When a community, large or small, wishes to discover and affirm the complex meanings in their history, they can use mythology as an instrument for interpreting, understanding and remembering it. Each person – desiring to explore the meaning, value and destiny of her/his own life - has an 'interior life' which waits for care and understanding. This is the foundation of a personal spirituality.

During the 20th century the term 'psycho-therapy' became familiar to many people. This discipline is based on the pioneering work of S. Freud and C.G. Jung in their studies of the human unconscious. A person's developing spirituality can profit from this work, especially in its interpretation of the dynamics of the interior life. But whereas psychotherapy is often practised for personal healing, spirituality has a larger task; it is usually faith-based and is orientated to both the present and the future.

> **When someone recognizes and desires to support an interior life, s/he can begin a dynamic spirituality that calls for a moderately disciplined lifestyle. The interior life is a result of the creative dialectic between personal being and personal becoming; it requires a 'discourse of the soul' which is necessarily symbolic. This process, however, is subject to stalling if the creative dialectic is not supported daily in prayer and responsible living. Then the interior life is diminished.**

(An 'End Note' on depth psychology, provided below, gives additional information about this discipline.)

Questions for discussion:

1. Exodus 6:2-7, 7:1-7 Which of these verses appear to be mythology? which appear to be history?
2. There are other categories of biblical text. How would you describe Exodus 12:1-20; Exodus 13:1-13; Mark 5: 1-20?
3. Each person has her or his own Story. From your memory bank of personal stories, recall an example of 'history' and 'mythology' and how the two relate.
4. How would you describe the contemporary mythology of technological society?

5

PROPHECY IN ANCIENT ISRAEL

> *The task of prophetic ministry is to nurture, nourish and evoke a consciousness and perception alternative to the consciousness and perception of the dominant culture around us.*
>
> Walter Brueggemann (The Prophetic Imagination, p.3)

Hebrew prophecy sought - through many centuries and many voices - to elaborate and guide ancient Israel's response to Yahweh's insistent requirements for personal and social moral life. Israel heard these moral standards in the oracles of her prophets as injunctions relating both to specific historical situations and also as part of an emerging ethical body of instruction for the nation.

> Hear the word of the, Lord, you rulers of Sodom!
> Listen to the teachings of our God, you people of Gomorrah!
> What to me is the multitude of your sacrifices? says the Lord;
> I have had enough of burnt offerings of lambs and the fat of fed beasts;

> I do not delight in the blood of bulls or of lambs, or
> of goats.
> When you come to appear before me, who asks this
> from your hand?
> Trample my courts no more; bringing offerings is
> futile: incense is an abomination to me.
> New moon and sabbath and calling of convocation –
> I cannot endure solemn assembly with iniquity.
> Your new moons and your appointed festivals my
> soul hates;
> They have become a burden to me, I am weary of
> bearing them.
> When you stretch out your hands, I will hide my eyes
> from you: even though you make many prayers,
> I will not listen; your hands are full of blood.
> Wash yourselves; make yourselves clean; remove the
> evil of your doings from before my eyes; cease to
> do evil, learn to do good, seek justice, rescue the
> oppressed, defend the orphan, plead for the widow.
> (Isaiah 1:10-17)

Seek good and not evil, that you may live; and so the Lord, the God of hosts will be with you. Hate evil and love good, and establish justice in the gate; it may be that the Lord, the God of hosts, will be gracious to the remnant of Joseph.
(Amos 5:14,15)

I hate, I despise your festivals, and I take no delight in your solemn assemblies. Even though you offer me your burnt offerings and grain offerings, I will not accept them; and the offerings of well-being of your fatted animals, I will not look upon. Take away from me the noise of your songs; I will not listen to the melody of your harps, but let justice roll down like waters, and righteousness like an everflowing stream. (Amos 5:21-24)

Come, let us go up to the mountain of the Lord, to the house of the God of Jacob; that he may teach us his ways and that we may walk in his paths. For out of Zion shall go forth instruction, and the Word of the Lord from Jerusalem.

He shall judge between many peoples, and shall arbitrate between strong nations far away they shall beat their swords into ploughshares, and their spears into pruning hooks; and nation shall not life up sword against nation, neither shall they learn war anymore; but they shall sit under their own vines and under their own fig trees, and no one shall make them afraid; for the mouth of the Lord has spoken. (Micah 4:2-4)

These well-known selections from three Hebrew prophets are examples of the biblical call for justice and compassion in all inter-human relationships. They represent major prophetic themes, some of which become evident much later in the public ministry of Jesus of Nazareth.

PROPHETIC WITNESS

It is customary in to speak of 4 major and 12 minor prophets. Hosea (mid to late 8th century BCE) was a minor prophet who lived in the northern territory of Israel, in the city of Samaria.

> When the Lord first spoke through Hosea, the Lord said to Hosea, "Go take for yourself a wife of whoredom and have children of whoredom; for the land commits great whoredom by forsaking the Lord.

So he went and took Gomer daughter of Diblain, and she conceived and bore him a son. (Hos 1.2-3)

It is significant that Hosea believed Yahweh had instructed him to marry a harlot. As the man Hosea struggled to be faithful to his unfaithful wife Gomer, Hosea the prophet was learning about Yahweh's desire to be 'faithful' to his 'unfaithful wife' Israel.

When Israel was a child, I loved him, and out of Egypt I called my son. The more I called them, the more they went from me; They kept sacrificing to the Baals, and offering incense to idols.

Yet it was I who taught Ephraim to walk, I took them up in my arms: But they did not know that I healed them. I led them with cords of human kindness, with bands of love. I was to them like those who lift infants to their cheeks. I bent down to them and fed them.

They shall return to the land of Egypt, and Assyria shall be their king, because they have refused to return to me. The sword rages in their cities, it consumes their oracle-priests, and devours them because of their schemes. My people are bent on turning away from me. To the Most High they call, but he does not raise them up at all.

How can I give you up, Ephraim? How can I hand you over, O Israel? How can I make you like Admah? How can I treat you like Zebobiim? My heart recoils within me; my compassion grows warm and tender.

I will not execute my fierce anger; I will not again destroy Ephraim. For I am God and no mortal, the

Holy One in your midst, and I will not come in wrath. (Hosea 11:1-9)

This human/divine dialogue within the heart and mind of Hosea exhibits beautifully his struggle to grasp the reality of 'compassion' as one of the central truths about the God of Israel.

PROPHETIC GRIEVING

During the 8th century BCE, the royal courts in northern Israel at Samaria and in southern Judah at Jerusalem were indifferent to immanent threats from Assyria on the east and from Egypt on the south. Both royal courts depended on diplomacy in the face of impending military defeats and social catastrophe. In response to this appalling national self-deception prophets spoke oracles calling their respective peoples to a return to covenant faithfulness. The prophets believed that without moral and spiritual renewal their nations would suffer catastrophic interior suffering, social collapse, and foreign invasion. Brueggemann demonstrates that the public oracles of the prophets Hosea and Amos (against Israel) and Micah, Isaiah and Jeremiah (against Judah) repeatedly used a certain kind of language in response to the dangerous circumstances of their people. He writes,

> I believe that the proper idiom for the prophet in cutting through the royal numbness and denial is the *language of grief*, rhetoric that engages the community in mourning for a funeral they do not want to admit to. It is indeed their own funeral... And I believe that grief and mourning, that crying in pathos, is the ultimate form of criticism, for it announces the sure end of the whole royal arrangement. If we are to understand prophetic criticism we must see that its characteristic idiom is anguish and not anger. (*Italics in the original.*)

(W. Brueggemann, *The Prophetic Imagination*, p.46)

Brueggemann also shows that the spiritual practice of grieving, in contrast to official optimism, was the energizing context for prophetic hope.

> Hope is the refusal to accept the reading of reality which is the reading of the majority opinion; and one does that only at great political and existential risk. On the other hand, hope is subversive, for it limits the grandiose pretension of the present, daring to announce that the present to which we have commitment is now called into question.
> (*ibid, p.65*)

Brueggemann also gives extensive attention to the early times of Moses when the Israelites were captive in Egypt. He recalls that the tradition emphasizes the "groaning" of Israel, the helplessness of a People under oppression. Yahweh "heard the cry of the People" and sent Moses to lead a grieving People from slavery into a new land.

In the next chapter, when discussing the gospels of the New Testament, I return to this subject of 'prophetic grief' in the context of Jesus' public ministry.

Questions for discussion:

1. What community moral standards were being urged Isaiah? by Amos? by Micah?
2. Which of these moral standards are urgently needed in our society?
3. What did Hosea learn about Yahweh's relationship with unfaithful Israel?
4. How would you describe the personal qualities of these men as prophets of Israel?

6

FOUR GOSPELS: TEXT IN CONTEXT

In recent decades, many people have been learning that the Bible is not the Word of God. Rather, they have realized that biblical texts are the words of devout believers attempting to share with posterity their many and diverse encounters with the Holy One. For us to engage creatively with and to learn from these many different biblical witnesses is challenging work.

Biblical documents, from Genesis through to the end of the New Testament, were developed during many centuries and by many people. These people lived in a wide variety of situations and with an even wider variety of presuppositions and commitments. In the Bible we encounter a plethora of historical, cultural and personal interests which shaped biblical texts as each was conceived, remembered, passed on, and ultimately written down. While these writings sometimes seem divinely inspired, they also give ample evidence of human questions, struggles and insights.

Some texts have enduring value and wondrous potential for us as readers and enquirers when they occasion a 'Living Word' in our hearts and minds. But the experience of receiving a Living Word can never be anticipated and initially it may only cause us to wonder. The authenticity of a Living Word is evident *when it addresses our personal, contemporary human situation with relevance and power.* A Living Word is always Spirit-driven, it is a 'graced moment' - though it can vary widely in degree of amazement, illumination, or confusion. And the movement from written text to Living Word is never entirely logical; it always holds an imponderable mystery.

There are other graced moments, Aha! experiences, which occur without the stimulus of a biblical text. These can happen within dynamic human relationships, in response to beautiful works of art, when we are alert to the natural world around us, etc. I strongly affirm these latter moments - but they are not my concern here. The intent of this chapter is to identify and illuminate some of the historical/social complications in first century Palestine which can cloud our reading of the New Testament Gospels. I suggest that if we recognize and allow for these historical/ textual complications we are better able to listen for a Living Word about Jesus of Nazareth.

JESUS OF NAZARETH - a prophet in Galilee

About 70 AD, the Gospel of Mark appeared in the Jesus Movement, forty years after Jesus' death. This gospel begins with Jesus going to Jordan River in response to John the Baptist's call urging Jews to prepare for the approaching Day of Divine Judgment. The Gospel of Matthew (c.AD 80) and the Gospel of Luke (c.AD 85) used Mark's general story-line, and each added substantial text of their own. The texts of these three 'synoptic' gospels came from three separate communities within the new Jesus Movement. John the Evangelist (c.AD 100) provides theological commentary on Jesus' person and work. The context of all four gospels was Roman Palestine, comprised of three distinct regions: Judea in the south, Samaria in the centre, and Galilee in the north. Judea was the largest region, being approximately one and one half the size of Samaria; Samaria was twice the size of the Galilee. The Sea of Galilee lay in the SE section of the Galilee.

The gospels were written in the colloquial *koine* Greek of that time and they tell many stories about Jesus' itinerant life-style during the last two years of his life. Mark and Matthew state that he was a *tekton*, which has usually been translated as 'carpenter'. However, today this word refers to a skilled craftsman - which makes this translation misleading. In Roman Palestine a *tekton* was an artisan

> below the Peasants in social class because they were usually recruited and replenished from its dispossessed members... since between 95 and 97 percent of the Jewish state was illiterate at the time of Jesus, it must be presumed that Jesus also was illiterate. (J.D. Crossan, *Jesus: A Revolutionary Biography, p.25)*.

Only the final two years of Jesus' life are reported in the gospels. What, then, was happening within his mind and heart in the earlier years when he was employed in menial work? In the gospels Jesus is shown constantly moving about as a highly-visible itinerant teacher and healer. Itinerants of different kinds were a familiar sight in those times. There were the 'cynics' who walked the roads, sometimes with a small company of disciples. These men travelled light. They were adept at cryptic sayings, stories and parables with an accent on attacking opinions different from their own. Their criticism was not directed just at the materialism of Hellenistic culture, it was directed more fundamentally at civilization itself. But there is no evidence that Jesus was a cynic.

There were also erudite and itinerant teachers called 'sophists' who developed reputations as learned men. They too were public debaters who sometimes established local schools. Though Jesus was remembered as creating an enduring legacy of brief sayings, and of longer aphorisms and parables, he was not a sophist.

Extensive critical research of the texts of the New Testament gospels has revealed that during the years c. AD 30 to 50 – the two decades before the first of our present four narrative gospels were written - some of Jesus' teaching was being recalled and shared orally among members of the new Jesus Movement *using the traditional skills of story- telling*. During these 20 years, some of those remembered and rehearsed events about Jesus were gathered into a written document of which we have no extant copy. However, proof of the existence of this very early document can be found by comparing parallel texts found in the narrative Gospels of Matthew and Luke. Scholars named this lost document "Q", from the German word *quelle* meaning "source". From Burton Mack we learn that

> many of the wisdom sayings of Q looked strange when compared with the maxims, proverbs and injunctions typical for the standard collection of wise sayings. There could be no doubt that these saying in Q were crafted in the forms of wisdom speech and treated as sage instructions. Many are aphoristic, delighting in extreme cases and in imagery that was more pungent and evocative than observational and instructive. And there was a very large imbalance in favour of imperatives, injunctions and instructions in specific details of behaviour... Something was being recommended other than the wisdom required for well- being either in a conventional society or in a well-informed subcultural group... Q's challenge to its readers was to have another look at their world and dare to dance to a different tune.
> (Burton Mack: *The Lost Gospel, p.45*).

I imagine the man Jesus moving among the villages of the Galilee for 10 or 15 years, earning his living as a *tekton,* and eventually becoming a recognized 'public person'. It seems likely that in those early years he was daily testing his emerging personal convictions for their potential relevance to the troubled society of his day. There are many allusions in his parables and sayings to problematic social and economic relationships present in that radically unjust society. This was a world of oppressive Roman militarism and restless Hebrew religious questioning. It was also a world saturated with an assortment of religions which over centuries had made niches for themselves throughout the Mediterranean region. The gospels occasionally reveal some of these cultural influences among the Galileans, but there is no reason to believe that Jesus himself was seriously interested in them.

We can assume that Jesus' spiritual life was embedded in a profound and continuing relationship with the Holy One of Israel. He was a *tekton* with a profound ability to understand and reflect on the minds and hearts, and on the social and economic circumstances, of his contemporaries. The power of his teaching is partly to be found in the coherence between what he said and how he lived. But it seems to me that there had to be more - something in addition to the words and deeds which were remembered and shared among the earliest disciples of the Jesus Movement. I think there must have been something unique *in the man himself*, a Presence, an aura, which forever transformed the lives of some of his listeners.

In contemporary Roman Palestine there was a widespread expectation among Jewish believers of a soon-to-come Day of the Lord which would fulfill all that the Law and the Prophets had anticipated. This expectation has been described as the yearning for an 'apocalyptic eschatology': a Revelation of Yahweh which would bring in the End Time. Recalling today that widespread Jewish expectation, we can imagine why at least a portion of the early Jesus Movement (with a powerful lead from the Apostle Paul) applied the term 'Messiah' to Jesus. In this manner he was being identified as the One sent by Yahweh to be his Suffering Servant: to release Israel from the oppressor's heel, and to heal the world of its sinfulness. The Apostle Paul gave his own summation of Jesus as Messiah:

"Being of the very nature of God, he assumed the form of a servant and humbled himself even to death on a cross. (*cf:* Phil 2: 6-11)

Some Christians today are unable to accept this messianic designation as a complete interpretation of the significance of Jesus: it gives no recognition to the Man himself, to 'Jesus of History'. For these Christians, Jesus of Nazareth demands new understanding and new ways of speaking about him. For them, new imagery/symbolism is needed to guide and support the faith journey of contemporary people. (My first glimpse of this possibility happened many years ago when I saw a Sunday School illustration of an Arabic-looking Jesus, laughing!)

Paul's words in his Letter to the Philippians represent one of the two early expressions of Christianity. J.D.Crossan observes:

> It is necessary, then, to distinguish two traditions in earliest Christianity, one emphasizing the sayings of Jesus and the other emphasizing the death and resurrection of Jesus… There should be no overt ascendancy of either over the other."
> (J.D. Crossan: *The Birth of Christianity*, p. 415)

CONTEXTUAL ISSUES

Memories about Jesus' words and deeds were treasured and collected by his contemporaries. Between 30 and 60 CE these core sacred stories were shared and shaped into units of written tradition and these units provided the early Jesus Movement with material for four Gospel portraits of the Master. These are not biographies; they are four interpretations and they differ from one another in many details. There have been attempts to harmonize the four Gospels into one story, but none has been widely accepted. Instead, the four must be seen as complementary to one another.

The three 'synoptic' Gospels of Matthew, Mark and Luke grew from personal memories of encounters with Jesus of Nazareth. These memories became the building blocks of an early oral tradition which by c.85 CE had received written form in the three synoptic Gospels. Each of these was the work of a community within the early Jesus Movement, each in a location which can now be surmised but not confirmed. (John's Gospel is distinct, needing special consideration.)

Memories about Jesus did not emerge within a placid or tidy social background where his message could be easily heard and understood. On the contrary: the activity of observing and listening to Jesus - and of remembering, retelling, and collecting those observations - took place within the tumultuous and difficult conditions of first century Roman Palestine. It was a time and place of harsh imperial oppression and exploitation, of onerous taxation of the peasantry, and of religious regulations imposed by Pharisaic custom and priestly temple rule. These forces resulted in widespread rural poverty, resentment and restless discontent - ultimately leading in the year 66 to civil war by the mass of Jewish people against Roman overlords.

The process of observing, remembering, sharing, and collecting the events related in the gospels was at first spontaneous and only later became organized. And in this random process details of the original contexts of Jesus' words and works were easily forgotten. (While Jesus was active among them, no one was planning to write a gospel!) Consequently, the persons who wrote the final texts often found it necessary to invent what they considered to be appropriate scenarios for the remembered material. Sometimes they inserted their own glosses into the text to supply a credible interpretation of Jesus' meaning.

The original, written gospel texts used colloquial Greek and had no verse or chapter designations; each gospel was one, single and continuous narrative. Each of the few existing early manuscripts has come to us as an integrated whole. Considering the unsettled social context, and that extraneous material and editorial work were often introduced by each evangelist, it is not surprising that the results are often obscure for readers. (Luke-Acts was originally one continuous story, telling how the Good News conceived in Galilee gradually travelled to the City of Rome.)

PARABLES AS SUBVERSIVE SPEECH

Readers of the synoptic gospels could easily assume that Jesus of Nazareth spoke his wisdom sayings and told his colourful parables to attentive and silent listeners. But this is very unlikely. Judging from historical records about other open-air teachers in the Roman Empire of the first century CE (such as Cynics and Sophists), it is virtually certain that when Jesus of Nazareth was speaking to groups of people he provoked public questioning and disputation. It is very probable that he generated energetic verbal encounters with his listeners.

The evangelists give examples of lively disputation when Jesus was in conversation with Scribes, Pharisees or Saduccees. But they rarely do so when reporting about Jesus speaking with close disciples or to large crowds of responsive people. These latter groups are usually portrayed as attentive observers and most times they are rendered silent, anonymous or invisible. On the contrary: Jesus of Nazareth was an engaging, challenging and receptive teacher, and his ideas and how he presented them were developed through dialogue with his listeners. One New Testament scholar makes this observation about the parables of Jesus:

> they were meant to be discussion-starters, whose purpose was to raise questions and pose dilemmas for their hearers. They were open-ended stories that invited their hearers to enter into conversation for the purpose of exploring the social scenes they presented and connecting the hearers to the realities of their

lives and the larger systemic realities in which they were caught. (Wm R. Herzog, *Parables as Subversive Speech*, p.259)

Among the three synoptic gospels there is much common material. Mark was the first to be written, used later by Matthew and Luke as a 'spine' for their own narratives. The gospel communities referred to as 'Matthew' and 'Luke' each had its own source of stories, and parts of these gospels came from another document of which no earlier copy exists (known among scholars as 'Q'). Moreover, each evangelist has distinct interests. For example, in the Gospel of Luke we see Jesus deliberately challenging some attitudes and expectations among his listeners. Here are three examples.

Luke 14:16-24 tells about a rich man who invites people to a banquet, many of whom decline with empty excuses. The rich man then sends his servant "to the streets and lanes of the city" to find the "poor and maimed and blind and lame" and to urge their attendance "that my house may be filled".

This is a surprising picture of an unlikely event in a society where an impenetrable barrier existed between peasants and the wealthy elite. In this story Jesus is being heavily rhetorical. Skeptical hearers would have had plenty of questions and comments about how this related to their own lives, especially the ending: "compel people to come in, so that my house may be filled". The parable is one of those which "raise questions and pose dilemmas" embedded in that society.

Luke 15:3-9 gives us the famous parables of the lost sheep and the lost coin. This also would have been an unrealistic picture for Jesus' audience. They were continually being pushed to extreme poverty by the exploitative practices of wealthy and powerful landowners, backed up by the presence of the Roman military. They knew firsthand what it meant to be forgotten and 'lost' and to drop off the bottom of the social ladder as expendables. But they might well have questioned Jesus on the relevance of his story to their lives and wondered about the true meaning of his mission among them. And notice how Luke altered the thrust of this parable by adding verse 10:

> Even so, I tell you, there is joy before the angels of God over one sinner who repents.

Did Jesus really wish to teach these people that they must earn God's love by repentance - or otherwise remain forever lost? Or does this comment echo the voice of an early Jesus Movement beginning to lay down conditions for newcomers to be accepted as converts?

Luke 10:25-37 gives the famous parable of 'The Good Samaritan'. The context is a discussion between Jesus and a lawyer about the commandment to love our neighbour as ourself. Notice how Luke the story-teller frames Jesus' parable within *two different questions*.

First the lawyer asks Jesus, "And who is my neighbour?" The lawyer wants a list which would imply that he is free to ignore other people. Instead, Jesus tells a parable about two community leaders who ignore a wounded man lying at the roadside, and one foreigner (Samaritan) who helps him. Jesus then asks the lawyer, "Which of these three, do you think, was a neighbour to the man who fell into the hands of the robbers?" Jesus names no one but instead asks the lawyer to say *who had acted as a neighbour*. "Go and do likewise." Be a neighbour wherever there is need. Jesus' listeners were being more than a little challenged by this parable.

An example of problems with a parable is found in Mark 4:3-8. The parable itself is straightforward.

> A sower went out to sow. And as he sowed, some seed fell along the path... other on rocky ground... other seed among thorns... and other seed fell into good soil.

Only the last seeding produced a good harvest. We can almost hear the people murmuring, "Which soil am I? How would I know? What should I be doing to improve my life?" The conversation with Jesus, could we have listened in, would have been intriguing. But Mark has nothing to say about this. Instead he has Jesus say later to his close friends,

> To you have been given the secret of the kingdom of God, but for those outside everything is in parables; so that they may indeed see but not perceive, and may indeed hear but not understand; lest they should turn again and be forgiven.

Was Mark trying to explain to his readers, about 40 years later, why some followers of Jesus were not experiencing 'the new life' in response to 'good news'? Are parables really meant to block our spiritual growth?

Each of the three evangelistic communities of Mark, Matthew and Luke had its own agenda, its own particular insights, interests and limitations. These qualities appear in how they contextualized or amended the sayings and parables of Jesus. We are wise to notice this and to compensate with our own questions and insights. Somewhere in our seeking there could be a Living Word.

SAYINGS, APHORISMS AND ASIDES

The three synoptic gospels report many pithy sayings, aphorisms and brief observations spoken by Jesus in his public teaching. Scholars identify these as having been originally small basic 'units of tradition' which emerged here and there in the early Jesus Movement. These small units (termed *pericopae*) became shared across the Movement and were gathered up by communities of believers who desired to create their own version of the sacred Story about the beloved Master.

Occasionally a small unit of tradition stands by itself, without any specific context. More often, sayings which had lost their original contexts but appeared to have a common theme, were gathered together into a setting contrived by an editor. The best example of this procedure is found in the so-called Sermon on the Mount, Matthew 5, 6 and 7, where we can often be puzzled by nonsequitors in the text. (Luke 6:17ff reports some of the same material, but comments that they were part of an open-air talk "on level ground".)

This problem becomes less troublesome if we challenge ourselves *to imagine what might have been the original and differing contexts* of these sub-groups of sayings. Sometimes we can 'enter' texts by using our imagination to watch Jesus speaking to his audience and then find ourselves in the picture. This kind of looking and listening is a process of 'living into the text'. This can be very revealing and rewarding if we allow ourselves to be taken beyond rational thought and to imagine/experience the impact on ourselves of watching or identifying with persons in a text. We can become present to people who were present with Jesus, and present to the Master himself. It is often revealing to notice our response to what we 'see and hear'.

JESUS OF NAZARETH'S GRIEVING

It is evident in the canonical Gospels that the first Christians placed emphasis on the crucifying of Jesus' body but in their stories gave much less attention to the prophetic grieving of his heart. And this emphasis on the physical crucifixion of the body resulted in neglect of his 'interior cross'.

> Jesus in his solidarity with the marginal ones is *moved to compassion.* Compassion constitutes a radical form of criticism, for it announces that the hurt is to be taken seriously, that the hurt is not to be accepted as normal and natural but is an abnormal and unacceptable

condition for humanness. (Brueggemann, *op cit p.88, italics as in the text*)

The crucifixion of Jesus was the direct result of religious, social and economic conflict in that society, conflict now well documented and assessed by historians. Jesus' words and actions were carefully formed responses to that conflict, his way of giving obedience to the Holy One. He was committed to the practice of justice and compassion in human relationships. He unmasked the arrogant pretensions and self-serving actions of the ruling classes; he challenged the established social code of honour and shame; he criticized traditional purity laws; and he encouraged the poor to become mutually supportive in caring communities. And all of this he embraced as his assignment under Yahweh, fully aware of the risks to himself.

Jesus was put to death by religious and secular authorities because, upon leaving Nazareth and after receiving baptism in the River Jordan, he took up the work of a prophet, healer and teacher. In his person and by his actions he proclaimed that the Reign of God had arrived. In the eyes of the authorities both Roman and Jewish, of the occupying power and of the temple establishment, he was first seen as suspect, later as dangerous, and finally as seditious – an enemy to the established social order who must be removed. The violent death of Jesus followed inevitably from the manner in which he conducted his public life.

If we are to appreciate the depths of Jesus' personal struggle as he participated in these critical times of the Jewish people, we must understand that in everything he did there was an interior cost. Given the external circumstances of his life, which largely determined the shape of his public actions, his commitment to the Reign of the Holy One was certain to bring him profound inner struggle and sorrow. When did Jesus' crucifixion really begin? When did the deep sorrows start? What was the cost he suffered daily for the mounting suspicion and rejection he endured as a result of his public actions? As we survey the gospels' public accounts of increasing opposition to Jesus by the authorities, we must speak of an 'interior cross' which he endured in his heart, a 'cross' of which the wood of Calvary was the ultimate and inevitable external manifestation.

Matthew 23:37 pictures Jesus looking over the holy city with love and grief:

> Jerusalem! Jerusalem! The city that kills the prophets and stones those sent to it! How often have I desired to gather your children together as a hen gathers her brood under her wings, and you were not willing!

Luke 19:41-42 speaks of the same event:

> As he came near and saw the city, he wept over it, saying, 'If you, even you, had only recognized on this day the things that make for peace! But now they are hidden from your eyes.

Both evangelists portray a profound anguish within the Master because of his beloved people. In Jesus' cry from the heart, they recall the agony which the Hebrew Psalmist had heard within the heart of his God:

> I am the Lord your God,
> who brought you up out of the land of Egypt.
> Open your mouth wide and I will fill it.
> But my people did not listen to my voice;
> Israel would not submit to me.
> So I gave them over to their stubborn hearts,
> to follow their own counsels,
> that my people would walk in my ways. (Ps 81:10-13)

There is a strong suggestion in the gospels that Jesus repeatedly had experiences in his public work which pierced his soul. We may imagine him walking the land with knowing eyes and a vulnerable heart. He was deeply moved by the injustices inflicted on the peasantry; his anguish and dismay would mount as he observed the spiritual blindness and resistance to his words and deeds by Sadducee and Herodian. And to all of this he returned understanding and personal grief.

There is a story about Peter Abelard, perhaps apocryphal but nevertheless revealing. Abelard was a monk of the medieval church noted for his great and wonderful teaching abilities but who was condemned as a heretic by the rigid and powerful ecclesiastical orthodoxy of those times. It is said that one day he and a student were strolling through woodland, deeply engrossed in conversation about the meaning of the Cross of Jesus.

The student was having difficulties understanding Abelard when they happened upon a large tree which had fallen across the path and which a thoughtful forester had cut a way through to assist travelers. Pointing to the separated trunk, Abelard asked the young man, "Where do the annual sap rings in the wood begin and where do they end?" The student replied, "They go from the roots of tree to the topmost branches." "And yet". replied Abelard, "they are only visible to us here at the forester's cut. The Cross of Jesus is like this cut. Though the depth of the divine grieving for humanity's sin is revealed in the Cross, like the rings in the tree it extends from human origins to the End Time."

DISCIPLESHIP TO JESUS

Exposing ourselves 'in depth' to Jesus of the gospels can help us experience something very important. The radical act which lies at the heart of discipleship is the decision of a person to attach herself or himself to the Teacher. Discipleship is rooted in a committed relationship to this outstanding person *whose presence is always more than his specific words and works.* It is possible to rummage carefully, again and again, through the deposit of stories and sayings in the gospels and to receive impressions of Jesus which reveal to us who he is, and not merely tell us what he did and said. We may learn to respond to Dietrich Bonhoeffer's famous question to Jesus, "Who are you for me, now?"

Though the gospels are not the Word of God, reading the gospels in search of Jesus is like roaming through a busy bazaar where there are many booths offering us somewhat random glimpses of his works and words. As we wander here and there, observing and listening to all that is being presented and trying to open ourselves to its significance, we might experience the presence of the Man whose life occasioned all these fascinating reports. This is the gift of a Living Word. This is a gift of the Spirit.

THE ENGAGED LIFE

The texts of the gospels are more than written records of people who were present to Jesus of Nazareth, early in the first century CE. They have always offered readers an opportunity to become better instructed about who they are in themselves, about their spiritual origins, and about their life's journey.

A Word occasioned in us by the Spirit – as listeners or readers to the gospels - is not an intellectual proposition, or an answer to questions of a theoretical nature. Our lives can be open to a Living Word when we are struggling with moral or spiritual challenges in our daily living, and enquire about them in the light of the Gospels. When we are committed to the engaged life, when we face life's questions and challenges with an open heart and mind and personal responsibility, we are open to a Living Word.

There is a beautiful story of the engaged life being intercepted by a Living Word in the biblical narrative about Elijah the prophet (1 Kings 18-19). This prophet of Yahweh had defeated prophets of the Baals in a public contest (18:30-40), after which he fled to the mountains in fear for his life. The reigning Queen Jezebel, a faithful adherent of the religion of the Baals, was furious with Elijah and had sent her servants to run him down and kill him. Elijah took refuge in a cave. The narrator continues,

> Suddenly the word of the Lord came to him: "Why are you here Elijah?" "Because of my great zeal for the Lord of Hosts", he said... The answer came: "Go and stand on the mount before the Lord". For the Lord was passing by... a great and strong wind... an earthquake... a fire... a low murmuring sound. When Elijah heard [the low murmuring sound], he muffled his face in his cloak and went out and stood at the entrance of the cave. Then there came a voice: "Why are you here, Elijah?... Go back by way of the wilderness of Damascus, enter the city and anoint Hazael to be king of Aram; anoint Jehu son of Nimshi to be king of Israel, and Elisha son of Shaphat of Abel-meholah to be prophet in your place."

Each of these commands represented for Elijah a challenging moral action to be accomplished in the Name of Yahweh. And note that they all involved public action. (A similar, colourful encounter story from the New Testament in found in Luke 19:1-8.)

In a previous chapter I wrote about stories in the Bible of divine/human encounter. Reflection on these stories can contribute much to our ongoing spiritual pilgrimage. These stories witness to the experience by open-hearted people of receiving moral and spiritual guidance, and healing of body, mind and soul. A Living Word was present for them to guide and support the engaged life. For careful readers of these dynamic stories, the words of the Bible are not 'the Word of the Lord'. But sometimes they open us to a Living Word which comes as a gift to enable a transformation in how we live.

In this manner the Spirit continues to sustain and guide the pilgrim community. Together we may contribute to a restatement of the Christian Story which some of the world is waiting to hear.

Questions for discussion:

1. Recall and share experiences of 'aha' moments – moments of special insight or joy.
2. What aspects of peasant life under the Roman occupation would Jesus of Nazareth be likely to have experienced?
3. Imagine Jesus telling one of his parables to a small gathering of villagers.

   What kinds of reaction would you expect to see?
4. Read Lk 15:3-9. How do you understand these two different ways of responding to Jesus' parable?
5. Compare Mk 4:3-8; Mt 13:3-8; Lk 8:5-8a. How does each evangelist interpret Jesus' teaching?
6. Compare Mt 6:43-48 with Lk 6:27-28, 32-36. What do we learn about each evangelist in these contrasting accounts of Jesus' teaching?
7. Where in the gospels do you see signs of Jesus' 'interior cross'?

7

APOCALYTIC ESCHATOLOGY

Perhaps the most important contextual factor, which influenced how Jesus of Nazareth was seen, interpreted and reported by his contemporaries, was the composite image of Yahweh God present in Jewish culture at that time. It is clear that Jesus, his family and neighbours were embedded in the daily life and religious practice of the District of Galilee. As indicated above, Yahweh God was understood to be the divine Creator, Warrior, Lawgiver/Judge and Covenant Maker in the midst of his People Israel. A further and late-coming image of Yahweh as Compassionate can be found in a few prophetic writings and some psalms. But this latter image counted little against the over-riding orthodox faith of the all-powerful, national Divinity of the four central images.

These five pivotal images emerged gradually in the several hundred years during which ancient Israel grew from tribal to national status. In teaching and ritual these images became blended. In disparate forms they appear constantly within Israel's oral and written traditions. And these blended images carried one central message. Israel believed herself to be warned that if the nation ignored Yahweh's Presence or denied Yahweh's Will they would risk present calamity and eternal loss. On the other hand, if the nation repented of her periodic apostasy then Yahweh would surely come to Israel as her deliverer.

About 250 years before the time of Jesus a compelling refinement of this blended image of Yahweh began to emerge among the Jews as a result of repeated national experience. Beginning in the 8th century BCE, Israel was overrun by a succession of imperial powers: Assyria, Babylon, Persia and Greece. During the Greek period, late in the third century BCE, a sect of devout Israelites fastened on the early Warrior image of Yahweh. They believed that Yahweh would soon be revealed in historical time and space to destroy Israel's enemies and vindicate his Chosen People. The long centuries of national tribulation were seen as leading up to an End Time (Greek: *eschaton*) of the final judgment. The Day of Judgment would take the form of a divine revelation (Greek: *apocalypsis*) bringing salvation to the Jews and calamity to their enemies.

In contemporary biblical criticism, *apocalyptic eschatology* signifies that among the ancient Hebrews there was an expectation that Yahweh would come in Judgment at the End Time to deliver his People Israel and to destroy her enemies.

Before and into the time of Jesus of Nazareth, anticipation of Yahweh's avenging presence and power had become a strong theme in Jewish religion. The biblical Book of Daniel written in the second century BCE is an example of this development. But the groundwork for a radical Yahwism had been laid by other prophets during preceding centuries:

> In that day the root of Jesse shall stand as a signal to the peoples; the nations shall inquire of him, and his dwelling shall be glorious.
> In that day the Lord will extend his hand yet a second time to recover the remnant that is left of his people, from Assyria, from Egypt, from Pathros, from Ethiopia, from Elam, from Shina, from Hamath, and from the coastlands of the sea.

He will raise a signal for the nations,
and will assemble the outcasts of Israel,
and gather the dispersed of Judah from the four
corners of the earth.
The jealousy of Ephraim shall depart,
the hostility of Judah shall be cut off.
Ephraim shall not be hostile towards Judah.
(Isa 11:10-13)

See, I am sending my messenger to prepare the way before me, and the Lord whom you seek will suddenly come to his temple. The messenger of the covenant in whom you delight - indeed he is coming, says the Lord of hosts. But who can endure the day of his coming, and who can stand when he appears? For he is like a refiner's fire and like fuller's soap; he will sit as a refiner and purifier of silver, and he will purify the descendants of Levi and refine them like gold and silver, until they present offerings to the Lord in righteousness. (Malachi 3:1-3)

During the Roman occupation of Palestine beginning in 67 BCE an 'apocalyptic virus' (my term) was spreading rapidly among the Jews, renewing a restlessness among the lower classes. Following the death in 4 BCE of the Jewish King Herod the Great, there were scattered uprisings of Jewish people in Palestine against imperial Rome. And for decades following there were sizeable Jewish revolts led by self-styled 'social bandits' (*cf.* Robin Hood) and 'prophets of Yahweh', and divinely-appointed 'messiahs'. These popular leaders and their followers looked with expectation for the Day of the Lord to come when Yahweh would destroy their enemies and begin an End Time of peace and prosperity for the Jews.

All these localized, open revolts were put down brutally by Roman legions. Nevertheless, this vigorous religious expectation continued to spread throughout Roman Palestine until 66 CE when almost the whole Jewish nation rose up and for more than four years engaged in civil war against Rome. When the war was over, the land was devastated, Jerusalem's temple was burned to the ground, about one third of the Jews had died and another third had fled the country. (A full discussion of these events is given in *"Bandits, Prophets and Messiahs"*, by Horsley and Hanson)

The first quarter of this turbulent first century CE in Roman Palestine was the historical context of Jesus' life and public ministry. During the last half of the century, when the New Testament Gospels were conceived and written, there was horrendous physical and social destruction and a desperate longing for divine intervention. As one result, many memories of Jesus' words and works became polluted by widespread messianic expectations circulating as an apocalyptic virus. Indeed, many members of the new Jesus Movement saw him as bringing in the anticipated divine apocalyptic eschatological closing of history.

APOCALYPTIC ESCHATOLOGY IN GOSPEL TEXTS

The voice of apocalyptic warning most familiar to church people is that of John the Baptist:

> You brood of vipers, Who warned you to flee from the wrath to come? Bear fruits worthy of repentance (Lk 3:7-8).

And there are other examples. Matthew 21:33ff reports Jesus' story about a landowner who took considerable trouble to create a fruitful vineyard. Three times he sent his agents and finally his son to collect the rent from the tenants, and each time the tenants repudiated or killed the messenger. The parable concludes with a question and an answer,

> When the owner of the vineyard comes, what will he do to those tenants? He will put those wretches to a miserable death...

The early Christian writers of 'Matthew' clearly imply that the landowner signifies Yahweh and the tenants signify stubborn Jewish people (not Christians) bringing upon themselves a Day of Judgment (i.e. total war).

In Matthew 11:20ff we are told that Jesus threatened three cities with total destruction.

> Jesus began to upbraid the cities where most of his mighty works had been done, because they did not repent. 'Woe to you, Chorazin! woe to you, Bethsaida!... And you Capernaum... it shall be more tolerable on the day of judgment for the land of Sodom than for you.'

This is the language of apocalyptic eschatology.

The Gospel of Mark, Chapter 13, is known as the 'little apocalypse' because it uses language consistent with that popular enthusiasm. Many early Christians who were Jewish by birth and training would have experienced the words and works of Jesus within that context.

This theme of an eschatological cleansing Day of divine Judgment and Salvation generated for many early Christians a belief in the Second Coming of Jesus. This is apparent in several texts of the New Testament letters. We meet it occasionally in Paul's letters, as in Romans 5:9:

> Since we are now justified by [Jesus'] blood, much more shall we be saved by him from the wrath of God.

This language reflects a contemporary Judaism infected with teaching about a wrath of God which was to come in the last days.

The most well-known Christian example of apocalyptic eschatology is the "The Revelation to John the Divine", the last document in the New Testament. Perhaps the most serious mistake made by the early Church was to include this writing in the New Testament. It skewed what succeeding generations of Christians believed about Jesus of Nazareth. And this problem was significantly compounded over the centuries as artists elaborated on the theme of messianic judgment in poetry, paint and music.

A DIFFERENT PERSPECTIVE

Apocalyptic eschatology was not adopted by all members of the Jesus Movement. Consider the report of his parable of a father and two sons, Luke 15:11-32. When the dissolute and disobedient son - now repentant - returns home, the father in love embraces the boy without any suggestion that he should be judged or punished. The father also reaches out with compassionate love to a second son who is resentful and angry at the generous welcome accorded his brother. The father embraces both boys with equal acceptance and unconditional loving. Indeed, this famous parable reads like a commentary on Jesus' saying,

> Love your enemies, do good to those who hate you, bless those who curse you, pray for those who abuse you. (Lk 6:27)

The same unconditional divine loving is even more apparent in Jesus' behaviour during his arrest and trial leading up to his crucifixion. If we ever doubted the total absence of retributive justice in Jesus' understanding of his God, it is abundantly present in these dramatic scenes of Jesus trial and sentencing for crucifixion. Jesus accuses no one; he extends his loving to even the most vicious of his adversaries. And nowhere in the narrative are we led to anticipate that any of them will suffer divine punishment.

In these definitive scenes we see in Jesus' mind and heart an unqualified image of the Sacred Presence as Unconditional Loving. There is no 'virus' here of apocalyptic eschatology to pollute his spiritual vision. And this is true in spite of the fact that elsewhere in their narratives the authors of the four gospels occasionally and mistakenly show Jesus as accepting some implications of apocalyptic eschatology.

'SUSPICION' WHEN READING THE GOSPELS[1]

The four gospels contain reports by people who after Jesus' death undertook to preserve and compile traditions about him. But in the gospels we are three steps away from his actual words and deeds. First is the step of people remembering as accurately as possible what he said and did; second is the step of transforming oral tradition into written units; and third is the work of collectors/editors of these units composing connected narratives. In each of these three steps human agents acted as 'filters', and human filters are never neutral. Each step in the formation of the gospels was affected by specific personal and social contexts within the Jesus Movement. In particular: recall that throughout this complex process all members of the early Jesus Movement were living with Jewish expectations of an immanent Day of divine Judgment - or later still, with confused thoughts and feelings following the destruction of Jerusalem.

A good example of the need for 'suspicion' in our reading of the Gospels is found in chapter 15 of John's Gospel. The words attributed to Jesus talking with his disciples resonate with our knowledge of his unconditional loving:

> "I am the vine, you are the branches. Those who abide in me and I in them bear much fruit."

---

1 E. Schussler Fiorenza (*In Memory of Her*)

But in the same text we are given other words attributed to Jesus:

> "Whoever does not abide in me is thrown away like a branch and withers".

This second saying is obviously not a quotation from Jesus. Biblical scholarship helps us to understand the background to this discrepancy.

KINGDOM SAYINGS

In the gospels there are more than fifty references to Jesus teaching about "the kingdom of God".

> Jesus went about all the cities and villages, teaching in their synagogues, and proclaiming the good news of the kingdom, and curing every disease and every sickness. (Mt 9:35)
>
> "If it is by the Spirit of God that I cast out demons, then the kingdom of God has come to you." (Mt 12:28)
>
> They were all amazed and kept saying to one another, "What kind of utterance is this? For with authority and power he commands the unclean spirits, and they come out!... But [Jesus] said to them, "I must proclaim the good news of the kingdom of God to other cities also." (Lk 4:36, 43)
>
> [Jesus said], "The kingdom of heaven is like treasure hidden in a field, which someone found and hid; then in his joy he goes and sells all that he had and buys that field." (Mt 13:44)

New Testament scholar John Meier affirms:

> By its coming into the present world through the ministry of Jesus, the kingdom sets up a certain field of force or realm of human existence in which the power of the kingdom is concretely experienced. Hence people are said to "enter into" the kingdom, to "be in" the kingdom, or to "see" the kingdom. (Meier, *"A Marginal Jew", p.161*)

In the gospels we are told that in response to Jesus' ministry some people experienced 'new life'. In effect Jesus was challenging the reigning mythology of an anticipated divine apocalypse and cataclysmic final judgment. He was emphasizing new life, now, not salvation in an apocalyptic future.

THE WAY OF THE SPIRIT

While some members of the new Jesus Movement looked for the world to end soon with the return of Jesus and the coming of his kingdom, most of his kingdom sayings imply a different expectation and interpretation. For example: sayings about the kingdom being like yeast in dough, like a highly desirable pearl of great price, like valuable treasure hidden in a field, or like a mustard plant which grows rapidly.

Some biblical scholars argue that by the term 'kingdom' Jesus was pointing to the on-going transformation of human relationships among people, sometimes termed 'realized eschatology'. This view suggests that the kingdom is being realized now whenever and wherever people enter into compassionate and just relationships with one another. If this is an accurate estimate of Jesus' meaning in many of his kingdom sayings, then we have a strong indication of his intention to challenge the current apocalyptic eschatology with his own lively alternative mythology.

Jesus' teaching about the kingdom recognizes that it is elusive, even as life-giving human relationships are often transient and uncertain. We can move from being creative to being destructive, and vice versa. The kingdom wanes or even disappears when we treat others with suspicion, dishonesty or enmity. On the other hand, the kingdom is being realized, is being made actual, as we are open and honest, generous and caring towards one another. And this implies economic arrangements which promote equity and justice for all.

First century Jews in Roman Palestine lived in the midst of imperial military brutality and economic plunder, and were subject to Sadduceen religious hypocrisy and extortion. In those desperate times Jesus stood out as one who invited people to live 'by the Spirit'. He is reported as saying that "whoever hears my word and believes in him who sent me has eternal life" - these persons already live in the kingdom. The Fourth Gospel explicitly affirms that followers of Jesus have new life in the Spirit. And soon after his death his followers became known as 'People of the Way'.

8

JESUS' ALTERNATIVE SPIRITUALITY

LIFE IN THE SPIRIT

Important clues to life in the Spirit are given in a lengthy discourse attributed to Jesus in John's Gospel, Chapters 13 to 17. This extensive instruction of the Twelve was probably composed c.95 CE by one of John the Apostle's younger associates living in the city of Ephesus, who also had the name John. In a long discourse, this John the Evangelist elaborates on John the Apostle's personal memory of the closing hours which Jesus spent with his closest disciples. In these five chapters, events which had taken place some 65 years earlier were being remembered and retold in a new and carefully constructed narrative.

Here are some key verses:

> 14:15 If you love me, you will keep my commandments. And I will pray the Father, and he will give you another Counselor, to be with you for ever, even the Spirit of truth... you know him, for he dwells with you, and will be in you.

> 14:26 the Counselor, the Holy Spirit, whom the Father will send in my name, he will teach you all things, and bring to your remembrance all that I have said to you.
>
> 16:12 I have yet many things to say to you, but you cannot bear them now. When the Spirit of truth comes, he will guide you into all the truth.

In addition to these texts, John 3:1-8 is important, especially verses 7 & 8:

> Do not marvel that I said to you, 'You must be born anew.' The wind blows where it wills, and you hear the sound of it, but you do not know whence it comes or whither it goes; so it is with everyone who is born of the Spirit.

The followers of Jesus are meant to be spontaneous and unpredictable in their lives - like the wind. These references in the Fourth Gospel to gifts of the Spirit suggest that this spontaneity is what we are to expect and to understand as signs of the kingdom of God among us. Life in the Spirit is open and undefined - like the movement of the wind. It rescues us from despair when human affairs go seriously wrong, when injustice and suffering assume appalling proportions.

PAUL'S LIST

The Apostle Paul, in Galatians 5:21*ff*, identifies nine *Gifts of the Spirit* which can be gathered into three clusters. The first three are foundations for personal/community spirituality:

LOVE: this sacred Gift enables each of us to recognize and value those unique and essential qualities which constitute who we are. While other people on occasion offer us their love, and by this love support our personal well-being, the divine Loving is constant and unqualified. It is enduring and dependable. And though it is known by us most surely within regular, prayerful desire and acceptance, there are amazing moments when this Love is unexpectedly given and accepted.

JOY: this Gift enables each of us to recognize and quietly to celebrate special events and qualities in our personal life. And there are other times when we celebrate the Joy present in the lives of other people.

PEACE: enables us quietly to possess, with inward contentment, the foundational reality of our person as one of the 'Beloved'.

The next three Gifts are discovered and practised within our relationships with others.

PATIENCE: this attitude and action extends an invitation to other persons to be present to us in their own uniqueness, without qualification. It also helps us to find satisfaction in our own mundane daily occupations.

KINDNESS: this Gift is a 'partner' to Patience. It honours the other person; it establishes them as both separate from us and valued by us.

GOODNESS: this Gift is the attitude and action which honour other persons as desirable partners in reciprocal, personal relationships.

The third group of three Gifts helps us be aware of our self as one of the Beloved.

FAITHFULNESS: enables us continually to renew an awareness of and relationship with the ultimate Ground of all Being, to be deeply present to this Sacred Presence.

GENTLENESS: enables us to avoid being violent toward ourself, not to make unreasonable demands on ourself, to be understanding of our own stumbling ways.

SELF-CONTROL: this is the 'guard dog' which watches over our natural desires and regulates them for our own and others' well-being.

CONTRASTING SPIRITUALITIES

The contrast between a future apocalypse of divine salvation and a present energizing kingdom of God has been reflected in the life of the historic church. Apocalyptic religion has fastened upon human sin, the need for repentance, and the promise of eternal salvation in the future. In contrast, the Good News of the realm of God continues to affirm an unqualified divine compassion and the gift of unconditional loving to sustain transformed life, now.

The tendency to favour apocalyptic spirituality has been dominant in the life of the church. One interesting indication of this bias is found in the traditional name given to Jesus' parable in Luke 15, the so-called 'Parable of the Prodigal Son'. This traditional name has caused countless generations of Christians to notice only one son - his sin, his repentance, and his salvation - and to ignore the relationship between the father and a second son who is trapped in stubborn self-concern. The core message of the parable is not found in the prodigal son but in *how the father extends his same loving acceptance to both sons.*

Perhaps this story should be named 'a parable of a father's unconditional loving for two different sons'. The traditional name and interpretation of this parable have underlined sin, repentance and salvation and have left unnoticed the invitation to everyone to take up new life in the kingdom – now!

A spirituality centred around Jesus as the One who saves us from our sins has been the rallying cry of Christians throughout the ages. The church has embraced a biblical apocalyptic eschatology with enthusiasm. And this spirituality of eternal salvation through Jesus has blind-sided the true Good News of the unconditional divine Loving with its invitation to take this Loving into all human relationships - now. Church history has been more a tale of promising salvation to repentant sinners and less a call for Christians to act in prophetic witness for justice and peace. Many Christians have been addicted to an ancient and misleading mythology and failed to hear Jesus' mythology of the realm with its revolutionary spiritual and moral vision.

The centuries between 400 and 1200 CE are often referred to as the Age of Faith. But the legacy of these centuries for the people of Western society has been less an invitation to take up a transforming personal faith in Jesus and more the proclamation of an obsolete first-century Hebrew mythology/spirituality.

Today, given that we live in an expanding universe where Earth is a small planet circling a local star, itself located within one galaxy among billions, there are urgent questions to ask of apocalyptic eschatology. Does it deepen and extend whatever we already know about the universe? Does it promote responsible living on Earth? Does it assist us to be open to the divine Mystery which constantly seeks to engage with human thought and imagination? Does it enable and support a morality of compassion and justice?

IN SEARCH OF A RELEVANT SPIRITUALITY

In order to include the full range of human experience and aspirations within human self-understanding, a relevant spirituality is essential, one which offers a fullness of truth and meaning for human life. And, for some of us, this spirituality will enhance our understanding of the significance of Jesus of Nazareth and the realm he promoted.

The traditional Saviour figure of apocalyptic spirituality is a product of a distant time and its cosmic imagination. Today it can only lead us down a blind alley. This image has no resonance with the cosmos described by recent centuries of scientific discovery. It can only be disturbing and misleading. And a relevant spirituality will help us to discard all anthropomorphisms relating to the being or nature of 'God'. It will assist us to find images of the Sacred which are liberating for our life journey.

A spirituality is needed now which integrates our best contemporary understanding of the universe and the place of humanity within it with our most profound intuitions of the Sacred. This spirituality needs to embrace the fullness of both the mystery of Nature and the mystery of the Sacred. I suggest that Jesus' spirituality of the Kingdom of God fills this need.

Questions for discussion:

1. Which of Jesus' images of the Kingdom appeal to you? puzzle you? energize you?
2. To what extent does 'realized eschatology' give you an adequate understanding of Jesus imagery?
3. What experiences have you had of being guided by the Spirit?
4. To what extent do you agree with the author's claim that the historic church has place excessive emphasis on human sin and its forgiveness?
5. What elements of human spirituality need attention today?

9

THE APOSTLE PAUL

Any attempt to restate Christian faith for the 21st century must take account of the enormous influence which Paul the Apostle has had in shaping that tradition throughout its history. In his teaching, Paul gave a central place to questions of sin, judgment and salvation, themes which he received from his Jewish inheritance:

> a member of the people of Israel, of the tribe of Benjamin, a Hebrew born of Hebrews; as to the law, a Pharisee; as to zeal a persecutor of the church; as to righteousness under the law, blameless. Yet whatever gains I had, these I have come to regard as loss because of Christ. (Phil. 3:5-6)

However, in spite of the central place of Jesus in his adult life, the resulting theology which Paul developed only partially modified his handling of the traditional themes of sin, judgment and salvation. And his teaching has hobbled Christianity from its earliest days.

A MESSAGE NOT UNDERSTOOD

In his apostolic travels Paul constantly sought out 'God fearers'. These were religionists (whether of Persian, Egyptian, Roman, Greek or other persuasion) who were impressed by Jewish ethical monotheism. They attended synagogue worship but declined to be circumcised or to become full members of the Jewish community. During his travels in Galatia some of these God-fearers were ready to hear his gospel of Jesus and received Christian baptism.

In his founding and teaching of this congregation, Paul thought that he had been explicit and convincing when he related his experience of the Good News of the grace of God in Jesus. However, following on his evangelical work there, other Christian evangelists had come to Galatia and persuaded his converts that salvation comes through doing good works of the Jewish Law.

When Paul heard this he was dismayed and angry. He wrote to the Galatian Christians,

> Foolish Galatians! Who has bewitched you, before whose eyes Jesus Christ was publicly portrayed as crucified? Let me ask you only this: Did you receive the Spirit by works of the law, or by hearing with faith? Are you so foolish? Having begun with the Spirit, are you now ending with the flesh? (3:1-3)

Paul calls these other evangelists 'false teachers' because they had persuaded his converts that strict obedience to the Law of Moses was all that was required to obtain their justification before God. He does not dispute the teaching that sinful Galatians needed this justification; his dismay and disagreement was over how this justification is to be achieved.

Paul insists that good works do not reconcile sinners to the righteous God. It is only in *accepting by faith* the gospel of the Love of God manifest in Jesus that our justification is accomplished.

That is: Paul moves beyond his Jewish roots when he announces the Good News of freely-given divine grace in Jesus. *But he holds to those roots by continuing to affirm the ancient Hebrew image of the eternal divine Judge.*

Paul believed that Yahweh presides over a celestial divine Court where to gain eternal life we must be 'justified by faith in Jesus'. In other letters to early Christian congregations Paul returns constantly to this theme of divine judgment against human sin, and gives central place to our need for 'justification in Christ' before this God.

We see this insistence on divine judgment, for example, in his Letter to the Church in Corinth:

> Do you not know that the saints will judge the world? And if the world is to be judged by you, are you incompetent to try trivial cases? Do you not know that we are to judge angels - to say nothing of ordinary matters? (1 Cor 6:2ff)

Paul is strongly wedded to the double theme of judgment and justification. And our justification before God will be won by personal faith in the voluntary death of Jesus on a cross - a death required by the Court to cancel out the consequences of human sin. Only by faith in the victory won by this death is humanity released from a necessary judgment on sin. (*cf* Rom 5:18-21)

This teaching became the basis for 'Atonement theology' in later church teaching ("Jesus died to save us from our sins"), a position which some Christians now find mistaken and obsolete. I contend that there is no place in Jesus' spiritual vision for the Sacred Presence as Judge. There is no place for a divine celestial Court where everyone stands as sinners condemned until they accept that Jesus 'died for us'.

THE PAULINE LEGACY

The much-respected biblical scholar Marcus Borg recently published a book titled "Evolution of the Word". This volume places in sequence all 27 documents of the New Testament according to their probable dates of composition, beginning with the earliest. As a result, in this book all the seven authentic letters of Paul the Apostle are placed first, having been written in the decade of the 50's of the first century. Then, following Paul's letters, we find the other documents including the gospels.

When we read all seven of Paul's letters in quick succession *as background to the writing of the gospels* we can recognize the overall impact of his theology upon the emerging Jesus Movement. It is evident that, as his letters were being shared among the various communities of new converts, Paul's interpretation of the significance of the life and death of Jesus of Nazareth became normative. His interpretation coloured how the stories about Jesus were heard and accepted. His Jewish doctrine of God would have been accepted and integrated into his teaching about Jesus.

Here are a few statements from his Letter to the Christian Community in Rome which are typical of his general theological orientation:

> For the wrath of God is revealed from heaven against all ungodliness and wickedness of those who by their wickedness suppress the truth (Rom 1:18).

> By your hard and impenitent hearts you are storing up wrath for yourself on the day of wrath, when God's righteous judgment will be revealed (Rom 2:5).

> There is no distinction, since all have sinned and fall short of the glory of God; they are now justified by his grace as a gift, through the redemption that is in Christ Jesus, whom God put forward as a sacrifice of

atonement by his blood, effective through faith (Rom 3:23-24).

Just as one man's trespass [Adam in the Garden of Eden] led to condemnation for all, so one man's righteousness [Jesus' obedience causing his death] leads to life for all (Rom 5:18).

During the last quarter of the first century CE and into the second, whenever early Christians listened to stories about Jesus, the available letters of Paul exerted their influence. In particular, the current Jewish apocalyptic eschatology echoed by Paul became a significant context for the development of those stories.

I have urged that every biblical text must be read and can only be understood within its own historical and cultural context. But as we try to assess the impact of *Paul's letters as a whole* within the emerging Jesus Movement, we are less concerned with individual texts and their immediate contexts and more concerned with the wide and deep context supplied by the general thrust of Paul's teaching. In his writings we see him using, selectively, the Jewish religious tradition as the context for interpreting the significance of Jesus. This is hardly surprising since he boasts in his Letter to the Philippians of his deep roots in Judaism.

Paul's interpretation of the meaning of Jesus' life and death spread rapidly throughout the emerging Jesus Movement and is particularly evident in the New Testament "Book of the Acts of the Apostles". His influence was so great that six of the New Testament letters now known to have been written by other people were attributed to him. Moreover, his interpretation of Jesus' significance continued to spread throughout the Christian church during succeeding ages. Paul's teaching provided the structure for the church's historic doctrinal sequence: Creation, Fall, Redemption, Salvation.

Fortunately for us, there is more to Paul than his questionable doctrine of God. The transforming power of Jesus of Nazareth was also in him. His letters to the churches were inspired by his newfound faith in Jesus and he offers a treasure trove of memorable texts to encourage Christian faith and life. There is profound teaching in Paul's letters which has been helpful to people seeking the Way of discipleship to Jesus, but we must be aware that his theology of the divine judgment and wrath is now an obstacle to faith.

Questions for discussion:

1. What is the relationship between Paul's profound sense of humanity's sin and his equally profound sense of the divine Loving which is expressed in 1st Corinthians Chapter 13?
2. If you engaged in dialogue today with Paul, what questions would you ask him?

10

REALM OF THE SACRED

Spirit speaks:
  with a grateful heart open yourself
  to the Realm of the Sacred,
  to the flowing Energies of Loving
Energies which seek to embrace, sustain and transform all life,
  the Realm where to be sensitive to weakness in others
  nutures compassion and mutual kindness is
  unconditional

THE COSMOS

During the last century and a half there has been a paradigm shift in our understanding of the natural order. Scientists have established that planet Earth has been gradually evolving for approximately 14 billion years, beginning in a supernova explosion from which comes our sense of space and time. Scientists working in mathematical physics and molecular biology have discovered that according to quantum physics no continuous motion exists. There is an internal relationship between the parts and the whole, and among the various parts, in a context-dependence. Things could apparently be connected with each other any distance away without any apparent force to carry the connection. The mysteries of planet Earth and of its place in the Cosmos go well beyond ordinary common sense.

The implications of this are enormous, including our understanding of the role that consciousness plays in all Nature. There appears to be a species of consciousness that is inherent in everything. This alters our understanding of the relationship between what we have habitually named as 'matter' and 'spirit'. Nature is 'alive' and completely interconnected in ways that are not yet fully understood. Human consciousness has a direct function in Nature. Many categories of our understanding of Nature (including human nature itself) are now considered provisional.

ENERGY FIELDS IN THE UNIVERSE

Scientists have learned to think and calculate in terms of energy fields present throughout the universe. They have identified four: gravity, the electromagnetic, strong nuclear and weak nuclear. Each of these fields is an important energy force throughout the known cosmos. Each of these is a constant factor in human existence. In recent decades Rupert Sheldrake, a British biologist and lecturer, has done extensive research in force fields affecting human behaviour. He describes a field as a non-material region of influence that structures the energy of our universe.

About four billion years ago life first appeared on planet Earth. The subsequent evolution of complex nervous systems provided the anatomical basis for elementary forms of communication within and among the emerging species. By about one and a half billion years ago the remote ancestors of human beings had evolved with a well-developed mammalian brain. This brain continued to evolve towards becoming a physical structure capable of rational thought. Thus a new and extremely powerful energy source - human thought emerged to contribute to the future shaping of the planet. Some scientists are now trying to understand the nature of this field which structures the energy of human thought.

In her book "The Field", Lynne McTaggart (2001) reports in great detail many experiments which employ the methods and models of physics, medicine and psychology to study the nature and function of a fifth field which carries and supports the energy of human consciousness. She reports that there is now extensive evidence of activity in the human brain which appears to have no identifiable physical source. There are "masses of excitation... without regard to particular nerve cells" (*The Field*, p.80). That is: we can detect a psychic energy without an identifiable source in the brain. The question being posed is: What can we say about the source and nature of a diffuse field which supports and carries human thought? The research McTaggart quotes suggests that this field is integrally related to 'consciousness' - but is not to be identified directly with normal thinking processes.

> What these thoughts [arising during experimentation] were leading up to was a model of consciousness that was not even limited by the body, but was an ethereal presence that trespassed into other bodies and living things and affected them as if they were its own (*ibid* p.128).

That is: in addition to the four well-known energy fields present in the universe there appears to be a fifth which is directly related to thought processes.

Humans are much more profoundly and mysteriously interconnected than we habitually assume. Some studies began to suggest that at a more fundamental level of existence, there is no space or time, no obvious cause and effect...

> that the universe exists in some vast 'here', where 'here' represents all points of space and time at a single instant (*ibid* p.164).

> Both in common experience and in physics, time has generally been considered to be a primary, independent and universally applicable order, perhaps the most fundamental one known to us. Now, we have been led to propose that it is secondary and that, like space, it is to be derived from a higher-dimensional ground, as a particular order... If consciousness is operating at the quantum frequency level, it would naturally reside outside space and time (*ibid* p.174-5).

McTaggart's book offers an extensive review of the work of recognized scientists which explores the existence and significance of a Zero Point Field, a field which is non-localized and universal. The already-recognized four fields closely approximate this characteristic of instantaneity. And accumulating evidence suggests that human consciousness is expressed within this fifth field, a medium for psychic events of inter-human communication and affects. Many of these affects have been known for centuries but have never before been given a rational basis. Human consciousness is much more complex than we have recognized in the past.

THE RIVER WITHIN

The image of spiritual life as a river is useful in suggesting its dynamic quality and is consistent with the central place in Buddhism of 'mindfulness'. This latter counsel urges us to be truly present to our immediate environment through focused attention. Mindfulness calls for an unusual degree of "attention and consent" - a counsel offered by French philosopher, Simone Weil. All these spiritual practices - reaching inward and reaching outward - enrich the interior gifts which are ours through consciousness.

On the back cover of McTaggart's paperback there is an interesting comment by renowned author, Arthur C. Clarke:

Science has recently begun to prove what ancient myth and religion have always espoused: There may be such a thing as a life force.

And in his important book, *Ideology and Utopia*, Prof. Karl Mannheim wrote,

> One may admit that human life is always more than it was discovered to be in any one historical period or under any given set of social conditions. Even after these [discoveries] have been accounted for there still remains *an eternal, spiritual realm* beyond history, which is never quite subsumed under history itself and *which puts meaning into history and into social experience*. (p.92, italics added)

I find myself asking: Since we are now known to participate in five fields, *is there a sixth field with which we are also engaged?* Is there a sixth field which is the ultimate 'Ground of Being' of which theologian Paul Tillich wrote? Is there an ultimate energy field which is Sacred and Personal but not a person? Is this field the source of a cosmic Community of Loving in which we are invited to participate as the ultimate purpose and destiny of our lives? If so, then this might be named the Realm of the Sacred.

BOTH PRESENCE AND REALM

It is the function of our greatest spiritual teachers (the Buddha, Lao-tse, ancient Hebrew prophets, Jesus of Nazareth, Muhammed, Aboriginal Elders, etc.) to lead humanity to an inclusive awareness of the Realm of the Sacred. As we expose ourselves to this Wisdom of the Ages we can also explore the territory of our own search for a deeper understanding of life. And occasionally in this work we come upon interior intimations of a co-incidence between a Sacred Presence and a Realm of the Sacred.

Evelyn Underhill, scholar and writer of the mystical tradition, uses language about the Sacred which suggests both a personal Sacred Presence and Realm:

> The doctrine of the Holy Spirit means that we acknowledge and adore the everywhere-present pressure of God; not only as a peculiar religious experience, not as a grace or influence sent out from another world or order, but as a personal holy Presence and Energy... It means God entering into, working on and using the whole world of things, events and persons; operating at various levels, and most deeply and freely in that world of souls where His creation shows a certain kinship with Himself. (The Golden Sequence, p.12)

She finds similar language in the writing of an 18th century mystic, Pierre de Caussade,

> Action Divine... I can make no step save within your unmeasured Heart. All which flows from you today, flowed yesterday. Your abyss is the bed of that river of graces which pours forth without ceasing - all is upheld and all is moved by you (*ibid* p.19).

Within the mystical tradition is a two-fold imagery of Personal Presence and Sacred Realm, analogous to the discovery in modern physics that the basic structure of energy/matter in the cosmos is simultaneously particle and wave. In the early nineteenth century, complications arose for the corpuscular theory of matter to determine whether the basic elements of the cosmos are perceived as particle or wave. This seems to me consistent with the mystics' sense of the Sacred as both Personal Presence and Realm, depending on which aspect is being experienced and/or described.

A POST-CRITICAL NAIVETÉ

A sense of the Sacred in everything was integral to human consciousness for most of human history. Anthropologists sometimes refer to this long period as the time of a primitive naiveté, a time when human capacity for abstract and analytical reasoning was still undeveloped and the human mind was immersed in a world of immediacy and mystery.

However, this naiveté which is evident in mythologies of past ages is now firmly behind us. Humanity has lived through several thousand years in which we have been learning to apply reason to virtually everything. We value our rationality highly and through it have discovered an exciting and rewarding ability for creative criticism. We cannot abandon this; but we can refuse to allow our high regard for this faculty to hold us back from a new depth of consciousness which is also available to us. We can adopt what has been termed a post-critical naiveté – a term I first met in the work of Paul Ricoeur. This second naiveté can release our thought and imagination from a sterile rationalism which blinds us from the reality of mystery in the cosmos.

RADICAL IMMANENCE

Given the new cosmology which contemporary sciences are elaborating, I suggest it is counter-intuitive to posit a 'God-out-there' in space. Contemporary science affirms an inclusive interplay of all the forces within the cosmos as one integrated whole. This comprehensive point of view can be seen to include the human experience of *the Sacred as being radically immanent*, as the Presence who creates and sustains and embraces the Whole as 'the Beloved'. We need mythological imagery of the Sacred to help us shape a new spirituality.

In his 'Introduction' to Teilhard de Chardin's "The Phenomenon of Man", Julian Huxley states that

> Pere Teilhard starts from the position that mankind in its totality is a phenomenon to be described and analyzed like any other phenomenon... His second and perhaps most fundamental point is the absolute necessity of adopting an evolutionary point of view... always processes or parts of processes. (p.12).

We know now that everything in the cosmos is interconnected and that boundaries are permeable. The cosmos is comprised of a nearly infinite number of specific entities which together form one dynamic expanding whole. And all of this is in a constant state of flux. The smallest packets of energy studied by scientists are simultaneously particle and wave, moving in constant interchange. Science speaks of 'fields' of energy within which cosmic forces interact creatively in the continuing emergence, maintenance, and dissolution of Earth in all its various facets. Ecologically-rooted language is needed to picture all of this as vibrant and imaginative.

Teilhard de Chardin sought new language by which to situate the Divine as omnipresent in this dynamic cosmos - not only within the phenomenon of humanity but also within every element and aspect of the cosmic evolutionary processes. To communicate his sense of the foundational Reality in the universe he writes about 'the Within' as the internal, sacred quality of everything. This is not pantheism; it has been named by some as 'panentheism'. The 'Within' is an open and fluid concept which invites constant and imaginative exploration, especially by people who seek a spirituality that is consistent with the dynamic universe.

The time when we could suppose that any part of reality could be grasped in simple, univocal terms is now gone. As we try to speak about our sense of the Immanent Divine, the old language stammers and stumbles in its awkward solidity. One result is that the insights and convictions - that traditional Christianity expressed in solid words with firm edges, in formal doctrines - now need to be reprocessed into open words and fluid language which invites free reign of our imagination. We must create a renewed language of faith and of related symbolic actions that are flexible and evocative.

SOLID WORDS AND FIRM EDGES

Articulation of the Christian faith tradition was gradually built up around familiar ideas and language. An effort was made during many centuries to give the language of faith a specific content and clarity. I think of words like Lord, King, Creator, Righteous, Saviour, Sacrifice, Judgment, Salvation, Almighty, Eternal – a treasure trove of sacred nouns. Our liturgies make extensive use of language which seeks to create a clear and safe haven for our minds and hearts.

Many people still find comfort and support in the solid words and firm edges which are found in church liturgies. But it is also apparent that the traditional language and imagery of these liturgies are not gaining many new converts among thoughtful people. And further, there is the huge question of what kind of new and creative spiritual practice might nurture people who are able and willing to change the way we live on planet Earth. Our present life-styles are slowly destroying the ability of Earth to sustain us.

SYMBOLISM WHICH OPENS US TO A RENEWED SPIRITUALITY

The language of Hebrew faith is strong on the use of verbs and light on the use of nouns. Rather than seeking to name who the Sacred 'is', these authors use verbs which suggest how the Sacred 'acts' in their history. Yahweh created Earth, gave laws, judged the unrighteousness of nations, pardoned sins, guided the nation through the prophets. This language is consistent with Near Eastern symbolism of that time.

In the New Testament we do not find physical descriptions of the man Jesus, but there are many verbs which tell how his followers perceived and named his actions and teaching:

nurturing, transforming, disclosing, quickening, wounding, desiring, hoping, asking, questioning, honouring, listening, cleansing, sustaining, finding, challenging, loving, yearning, grieving.

A central challenge for spirituality today – and for this Primer – is to discover symbolism which can both engage with cultural norms of the 21st Century, and makes relevant use of biblical imagery of the Sacred Presence.

Which symbols will open us to the Sacred – words, music, visual form and colour, dance and drama – and take us beyond the range of our rational powers? Carefully designed spiritual practice is needed which provides us with these symbolic gateways between the human and the Divine. Using various media, we can search for depths of meaning and values to serve as spiritual foundations of human existence. And in doing this work we shall learn gradually that the Sacred Presence is constantly engaging with and assisting our efforts.

Today we live in a vibrant secular culture which daily uses symbolism drawn from a new cosmology, and from Earth's dynamic evolutionary processes, to seek roots for human spirituality. Available also are recent insights into the structure and content of biblical documents, which is one purpose of this 'Primer'. Using these resources we face the task of fashioning spiritual practice for creative ways to live on planet Earth.

In accepting this challenge we also engage with the huge question of what kind of new and creative spiritual practice is needed to nurture people who are able and willing to change the way we live on planet Earth. Our present life-styles are slowly destroying the ability of Earth to sustain us.

> *By bringing forth the planet Earth, its living forms, and its human intelligence, the universe has found, so far as we know, its most elaborate expression and manifestation of its deepest mystery.*
>
> *Thomas Berry*

Questions for discussion:

1. Discuss the appropriateness of 'field imagery' as a context for exploring the human sense of the Sacred.
2. To what extent is it helpful to image human consciousness as 'a river within'?
3. Name aspects of human spirituality important to you.
4. Which of these aspects do you think most need encouragement and further exploration?
5. Suggest 'soft-edged' words which might be appropriate for naming and guiding spiritual life in the 21st century.

11

ABORIGINAL WISDOM

In 1889 a volume of essays was published in England under the title *Lux Mundi* - "Light of the World". The authors were a group of leading thinkers in the English Church whose aim was to enter into dialogue with "new social and intellectual movements" of that time. They were inviting traditional Christians to listen in an open-minded and thoughtful manner to secular society's new intellectual currents, especially in geology, biology and physics. Today there is an equally valuable opportunity for Christians to learn from Aboriginal wisdom.

ORIGINAL SANCTITY

> "In the spring of 1992, as an Assistant Crown Attorney, I flew into a tiny Aboriginal village in northwestern Ontario to do court. On the docket were over twenty children, all of them accused of 'consuming intoxicants' contrary to the band bylaw... What was I supposed to do with these children in criminal court? Fine them? Make them perform community service work? send them to jail?"

These words of Rupert Ross from his book, *Returning to the Teachings,* dramatize the kind of dilemma he faced as an agent of Western legal practice delegated to court duty among Aboriginal Canadians. A basic premise of Western law is that accused persons must be given a fair trial and, if found guilty, be assigned punishment which is considered to be commensurate with their particular offense and likely to deter further transgressions. But when Rupert Ross arrived over 30 years ago among First Nations communities in Northern Ontario, he experienced a serious disconnection from his own legal education and training.

Fortunately for Canada, Rupert Ross was no ordinary representative of Western legal practice. Taking up his new work he became a careful student of Aboriginal society in its struggles with ongoing cultural, social and political problems. He began to understand how this People - denied access by Canadian government policy and law to their own traditional teachings and rituals - had accumulated deep-seated human problems in their communities. He also became a sympathetic observer of how the Elders, living custodians of the ancient ways, were slowly leading their people to a 'returning to the teachings'.

Ross describes how Western legal practice looks for appropriate ways to reform offenders through selective punishment, usually through incarceration under supervision. But Ross learned that traditional Aboriginal justice had never proceeded this way. For centuries they had expected children to learn by example and gentle instruction how to be functioning members of extended family life, both on the trap-line as well as in other aspects of community life. In this context they would see that to fail in one's personal responsibility could easily be life-threatening to the entire group.

Young people were encouraged to learn personal responsibility by observing how it functioned within their community. A sense of responsibility to the community was to be absorbed by them like the rays of the sun. Whenever there was an offense, the community as a whole accepted responsibility for the rehabilitation or, in rare cases, banishment of the offender. All of this community practice is embedded in the traditional teachings.

The aggressive incoming of European culture gradually undermined these traditional ways. Beginning in the mid-nineteenth century there was in Canada an official and concerted attempt by Government to eradicate 'Indian-ness' and, among other actions, to impose Western court procedures for dealing with offenders. The traditional stability of First Nations communities was gradually eroded. Social and personal confusion became widespread and Canada's jails received a disproportionate population of demoralized First Nations people.

Rupert Ross tells how he collaborated with Elders faced with offenders and for whom they sought to reclaim the traditional ways. Working in 'sentencing circles' he became a close observer of an alternative process to administer justice. He discovered that offenders were seen as wounded members of society who could be rehabilitated by teaching and healing and who, in their turn, became able to teach and heal others. In his books he sets out modestly to share what he has learned.

One of his major discoveries was that Aboriginal life has from its beginnings been rooted in a sturdy belief in the Good Creator and in a good creation. Every creature is a treasured member of the natural order; each person a treasured member of his or her clan. In his book *Dancing with a Ghost* Ross reports that the Elders seem to do their best to convince people that they are one step away from heaven instead of one step away from hell. They define their role not within anything remotely like the doctrine of original sin but within another, diametrically opposite doctrine which might be called the doctrine of original sanctity.

Ross points out that our Western legal practice regards offenders as 'bad people' needing to be punished. The Aboriginal system, by contrast, sees offenders as 'good people' needing to be forgiven, healed and instructed in better ways of living. The Western system tends to be punitive and the Aboriginal system desires to be restorative. Gently, compassionately, Rupert Ross in his writing offers for our consideration some of the teaching and practice that he has gained from Aboriginal wisdom. In particular, this wisdom stresses understanding, forgiveness and healing as the best response to moral failure.

ORIGINAL SIN

There is a profound difference in teachings about human origins between Aboriginal wisdom and Western Christianity, and this difference affects legal practice. Western legal practice draws substantially from an element in Christian teaching which began with Paul the Apostle and was reinforced by Augustine of Hippo and Martin Luther. This teaching stresses the biblical story of an Original Fall from grace by Adam and Eve and their resulting acquisition of a profound moral defect, a defect which every person inherits at birth. Each of us, Augustine taught, must acquire "the contempt of self" which only the love of God can redeem and which allows us to build "the heavenly city".

Church teaching about the birth contagion of original sin, and about our need to develop a strong 'contempt' of the sinful self, has had an uneven history in Christianity. Following early centuries of church life under the shadow of Paul and Augustine, the medieval church softened somewhat its teaching about sin. With its social roots predominantly in agriculture and the good earth, medieval Christianity developed the spirituality of sacramentalism. A sacrament "is an outward and visible sign of an inward and spiritual grace". Matter is a vehicle of Spirit. Seen In this context, even the Fall of Man was believed to have yielded the greatest prize of all - as we find in this interesting text from the Mass for Holy Saturday:

happy fault ! which has earned such a mighty Redeemer !

There was a creative tension in medieval Christianity which tried to balance the sinfulness we experience in our nature with the wondrous Gift of the divine Loving. On the whole, Catholic medieval theologians were optimistic rather than pessimistic about human nature.

It was John Calvin, and subsequently English Puritanism, which seriously undermined this medieval creative tension and burdened Reformation Christianity with a heavy conscience. Due to a Calvinist element in the Reformation, drawn from Paul and Augustine, sin and sinfulness received increased attention. For example, tales of the Kirk in 17th and 18th century Scotland, and of the Puritans in New England, are rife with harsh condemnations and disciplines visited upon sin and sinners. And Christian Baptismal rites shaped by the Reformation continue to instruct believers that we have all inherited the curse of the Fall.

A CONTEMPORARY CHALLENGE

Three insights into human behaviour, coming from the social sciences of recent decades, have abolished for many people this dark perception of human nature.

First, there is the contemporary understanding that human nature evolved during the last million years or so as part of the natural processes of planet Earth. Evolutionary anthropology finds no place, and has no need, for an event (or events) equivalent to the biblical Garden of Eden story and a derivative doctrine of Original Sin.

Second, depth psychology has revealed that the human psyche includes strong unconscious elements which affect profoundly how we behave. Our rational powers are complemented by non-rational feelings and insights, and by psychic wounds, which constantly influence how we relate to the world around us.

Third, sociological studies remind us that we are social animals. From the moment of our birth, the cultural forces of family, school, neighbourhood, religion, class, race, etc. mold our thoughts, feelings and actions. Personal attitudes and behaviour emerge from a complex of many factors.

From these three well-respected contemporary estimates of the sources of human behaviour we learn that the interior processes which shape our moral choices and actions are multiple and complex. Sometimes we are able to discern and name accurately certain of our actions as 'sinful', i.e. that we are morally responsible for a particular action. Often, however, this determination is problematic and unhelpful. Consequently, it is best to be careful rather than off-hand in making moral judgments about personal behaviour - both our own and others. Especially it seems unwise to speculate about a state of original sin and better instead to propose, with Aboriginal People, an original sanctity which becomes tarnished in the strains and stresses of living.

The Christian church needs to rethink its inherited and persistent preoccupation with sin in personal life. Why, for example, must we so regularly include the confession of sins in our public liturgies? Why do we not rather acknowledge in our liturgies our need for spiritual healing? Suppose, instead of repeated acts of confession, we made a point of celebrating the creative possibilities of human nature and also took care to name more directly the social ills and injustices that injure us all? The church needs to change its teaching about the significance of the Sacrament of Baptism with its peculiar perspective on original sin.

Questions for discussion:

1. From what sources does Aboriginal wisdom come?
2. Can you think of examples, other than expressed here, of ways in which Western culture can benefit from Aboriginal wisdom?
3. What do you consider to be the significance of Christian Baptism?

12

GOSPEL, LAW AND ADMONITION

The term 'divine grace' refers to the interior wisdom and strength which energize everyone's spiritual life. Theologians make a distinction between 'habitual grace' which is constantly ours by virtue of our creation and of which we are generally unaware, and 'actual grace' which we experience in unusual moments of spiritual awakening.

GOSPEL MOMENTS

I use the term 'gospel moment' to signify an event, unanticipated and unannounced, in which we recognize and accept for ourselves a Gift of unconditional Loving. These wonderful moments in our ongoing personal formation are times of actual grace. The less we feel worthy to receive such a Gift, the more amazed we are at receiving it. *A gospel moment always brings unaccountable blessing.* It can occasion a deep and creative change in how we feel, think and act. There are people in every time and place who have this kind of experience, mediated within a wide variety of situations.

Many stories in the New Testament report transformative gospel moments. e.g. Mt 9:20, Mk 7:26, Lk 19:1, Jn 4:7. These were events in which people recognized and accepted unconditional Loving as a gift of the Sacred, mediated by Jesus of Nazareth. Thus the term 'actual grace' came early into the emerging vocabulary of the Jesus Movement.

LAW

Law, in contrast to gospel moments, is usually prescriptive and has the feeling of an external power placing a demand upon us. Humans have constantly designed laws which carry a threat of punishment for disobedience. Laws are devised by ruling classes to control underclasses, priesthood to control believers, men or women to control one another, adults to control children, employers to control workers, etc. etc. When possible, we tend to ignore or deny a law when its demands seem unreasonable or unjust.

Hebrew scriptural teaching about Yahweh's Law, which included divine punishment for human disobedience, was widespread in the Jewish society of Jesus' day. In their stories about Jesus, the first disciples (almost all of whom were Jews) occasionally attributed this kind of teaching to the Master. Sometimes this attributed teaching referred to the final Judgment in the End Time; sometimes it showed Jesus judging and forgiving individual wrong doing. But these reports say more about views of the gospel writers than about the man Jesus. The divine Loving which Jesus taught and lived was *unconditional*. It was outside and beyond the realm of law.

At the time of his trial and execution, Jesus' refusal to condemn the men and women who themselves condemned him reveal most clearly his Gospel of the divine Loving. In the trial scenes others judged him as they scrambled to discover appropriate legal sanctions; but he judged no one. His sorrowing heart reached out to those who rejected him and had him executed. In the crucifixion scene we see Jesus offering these people the possibility of a moment of actual grace - and it appears to have been refused by most of them.

ADMONITION

In distinction from and in contrast to law, admonition provides welcome guidance for our thoughts and actions and does not bring punishment when ignored. Admonition has the feeling of good advice. In the gospel narratives Jesus frequently offers admonition to encourage creative living. These are found in wisdom sayings, aphorisms and short stories. And these admonitions must not be confused with gospel moments in which persons who encountered Jesus experienced his unconditional loving. Good advice mediated by admonition is not Good News - admonition seldom has power to transform our lives.

THE CHURCH AND LAW

Unfortunately, church teaching throughout the ages has usually portrayed Jesus as the compassionate agent of a law-giving God who as the divine Judge administers punishment to sinners and forgives those who repent. Disastrous consequences have come upon individuals and societies as a result of being trained to follow this church-inspired regimen of law, judgment and punishment (or forgiveness). Moreover, this legalistic church practice imported into the Christian religion the alien element of fear. And this regime of 'the fear of God' contrasts sharply with words of Jesus of Nazareth:

> If you love those who love you, what credit is that to you? Even sinners love those who love them. If you do good to those who are good to you, what credit is that to you? Even sinners do that. And if you lend to those from whom you expect repayment, what credit is that to you? Even sinners lend to sinners expecting to be repaid in full. But love your enemies, do good to them, and lend to them without expecting anything back. (Lk 6:32-5)

Jesus had a clear vision and open practice of the divine, unconditional Loving, a Loving dramatically illustrated (for example) in Jesus' well-known parable of a father and two sons (Luke 15:11-31). Throughout the New Testament the theme of divine Loving is central. And it contrasts sharply with the other and equally evident biblical theme of divine judgment and punishment. These opposing themes can be seen as causing a continuing contradiction within the evolution of Christianity, a contradiction which must now be left behind as a serious obstacle to understanding and living spiritual life in the future.

MORAL LIFE

The term 'sinner' came into the ancient Jewish tradition as naming a key element in their narrative about human disobedience to the Will of Yahweh. From there this term was taken into Christian teaching (strongly supported by the influence of Paul) and became accepted as part of the teaching of Jesus of Nazareth. To the contrary: this is church teaching which can now be seen as misleading and not consistent with Jesus' practice and teaching.

Human judgments and moral actions which intend well-being for others have their origin and significance in the normal intercourse of human life. But even our best moral efforts can result eventually in undetermined consequences which, through no fault of our own, yield situations of moral compromise or moral failure. Good intentions do not necessarily guarantee good results; history constantly records harmful actions consequent upon well-intentioned thoughts and deeds.

Though perfect moral insight and action is not given to humans, this does not mean that we are in essence 'sinners'. I believe that the Holy One never regards anyone as 'essentially sinful'. The amazing fact is that, regardless of our actions, we are always 'beloved persons'. Each of us is constantly being invited to accept the gift of the divine loving – without reservation or qualification. *To reveal this unqualified Gift is the true significance of Jesus Nazareth.*

There is, however, an important reason for each of us, personally, to accept the term 'sinner' as a recognition of our unavoidable failures in moral struggle. Literally the term sin means *missing the mark.* But in questions of morality there is no divine Accuser. We can recognize and repent of the immoral consequences of our actions. And we can be sustained in our desire to act morally by our awareness of the constant, generous, divine Loving that is our's with its unconditional Gift of amazing grace.

Questions for discussion:

1. Give examples of your experience of 'moments of grace'.
2. In what ways can our experiences of 'law' in daily human intercourse be creative?
3. Give examples of 'admonition'.
4. What feelings are involved in the offer and acceptance of forgiveness?

13

EGO, SOUL AND SPIRITUAL LIFE

The biblical reason for examining one's inner life or heart is that God knows what occurs there and cares about it. What God knows and cares about has importance for us. In the biblical tradition, and in the Christian history influenced by it, there is special and distinctive attention to motives. It is not enough that actions be overtly virtuous. It is equally important that they be performed out of righteous motives, especially love. To examine our own motives is not a pleasant experience, since at best we find them quite mixed. Indeed, a serious sense of sin and of our powerlessness to free ourselves from sin arises precisely when we examine ourselves in this way.

(John B. Cobb, Jr., *Process Theology*, p.141, ed. C. Robert Mesle)

Each of us experiences our mind as an intricate network of complex mental functions, one of which is ego. The ego function is central to that person/self whom we experience in a multitude of relationships with both Nature, other humans and with the Sacred Presence. Healthy human development is dependent in large part upon a healthy ego function. It is the foundation of a creative personality - but more than ego is needed to fulfill the human journey.

The anthropologist Loren Iseley writes that in 1908, in a small French cave, the remains were found of people who

> laid down their dead in grief... down the untold centuries the message had come without words: 'We too were human, we too suffered, we too believed that the grave is not the end. We too, whose faces affright you now, knew human agony and human love'.
> (*The Firmament of Time*, p.113)

This discovery (and others like it) indicates the presence of a psychic function more recently evolved in the human brain than ego, and which may be named 'soul'. Through the function of soul we formulate questions about personal meaning and destiny beyond death. Through soul we can be conscious of the Realm of the Sacred. And soul, in partnership with ego, enables us to build mature relationships with the world around us.

EGO AND SOUL

The physical basis for ego in humans came through the evolution of specific structures of the mammalian brain, itself an evolution from earlier structures of the reptilian brain. This physiological development in humans represented a huge step forward in cosmic evolution; it resulted in reflective human self-consciousness.

In addition to the human brain providing this genetic, physiological basis for consciousness, a fully developed human personality is also a product of relationships with Nature and with other people. From infancy a healthy ego is being supplied with an increasingly rich assortment of impressions, thoughts and feelings as the stimulating context for its creative development. Drawing upon both nature and nurture, our ego function gives us a sense of self; it allows us to know the 'I, me, and mine' in relation to the world around us. Ego not only facilitates our relationships with the external world, it makes claims of ownership in relation to various aspects of our environment. Ego activates a desire to feel 'rich' and 'important' through its relationships with people, things and places, as well as through personal attributes, knowledge and skills.

When we make the effort to monitor our mental processes, we notice ego as that function which seeks to foster, guard and advance what we feel to be our personal interests and well-being. And we might also notice another interior 'voice' which questions this ego work, a voice which challenges the central importance of self and urges actions for the well-being of other people. This second voice is an expression of 'soul'.

Soul urges us to practice the 'disinterested virtues' of selfless living. (Animals can have concern for other members of the same species, but this appears to be biologically rooted and is always partly 'self-interested'.) In distinction from ego, soul in the human seeks to create relationships with the external world which are self-transcending - attitudes like respect, appreciation, service and love. This is evident, for example, in actions such as generosity and compassion. Moreover, the coming of soul to human nature bestowed upon us a wondrous capacity for communion with the Realm of the Sacred.

Soul seems to be sequential to ego in the evolutionary process as a special gift of the Realm of the Sacred. Soul places humanity (and perhaps some animals?) in a cosmic context and seeks to release us from narrow egocentric existence. Soul complements ego by urging the self towards a wide and rich view of life. Neither ego nor soul is a 'substance'. They are mental/spiritual functions which allow the maturing self to grow in wisdom and to have opportunity to choose a path for her or his own life.

EGO AND SOUL IN TENSION

As the individual person matures, ego guards and seeks to deepen the search for self-realization. In this work ego supports a powerful self-centredness which can have difficulty offering respect and love for 'the other'. Ego experiences questions and challenges from soul which spring from its concern for others. Facing soul's selfless intention and activity, ego can become a false knave seeking to harness the self to our instinctual/animal past and to refuse our spiritual calling.

The origin of this tension between ego and soul might be expressed in this way. Ego is constantly building relationships within the natural order which the growing person needs for her/his personal growth, and in the process *inadvertently develops a degree of egocentricity*. Soul, in contrast, is the function within the psyche which encourages us to accept other-centred gifts of the Spirit such as "love, joy, peace, patience, kindness, goodness" (Paul, in Gal 5:21). It is the work of soul to place the essential work of ego in a large and creative context - a context of 'the whole', of both self *and* others. Soul can do this work for the self because it is a channel of the interior Light of the Sacred.

Soul work is advanced when we decide deliberately to practise the disinterested virtues of compassionate living. Ultimately, this disinterested work is essential for the full development of the growing person, for the realization of a person's spiritual truth and well-being. And it is at least arguable - if not considered obvious - that the practice of the disinterested virtues is essential if humans are going to succeed in living creatively together on Earth. Both among ourselves - as well as in our dealings with Earth itself and with her other creatures - we will fail in our evolutionary task if we do not grow beyond a consuming egocentricity.

THE SELF AND ITS PERSONAE

Each social location of our life asks from us an appropriate *persona* - a specifically limited and social expression of the hidden, personal self. Each persona enables a specific mode of behaviour which permits us to be comfortable and creative in a given social location: as a member of our family group, in a school classroom, in a place of employment, in situations of general sociability, etc. Thus, the development of these practical and public personae allows us to function as mature adults within the great variety of situations of life where many different kinds of behaviour are necessary. In this way we become able to express our potential as creative social beings.

We might say that soul desires to be 'active as a partner' with ego in the fashioning of these personae. Insofar as this fashioning employs both ego work and soul work, this partnership challenges a dominant egocentricity and works to include elements of selflessness in our relationships. On the other hand, because ego frequently and strongly resists soul work, we can experience inner confusion and contradictory feelings over what actually is appropriate social behaviour.

Is it possible to come to a time of life when an unrestrained ego can be trusted to do its creative self-realizing work and not block the soul work of spiritual growth? Or does ego always require watching and restraining so that disinterested urgings of soul can be expressed in our relationships? Writings of spiritual teachers of the ages don't encourage me to look for a time in my life when ego can be left unwatched and unrestrained!

MORAL AND SPIRITUAL GROWTH

In the Christian tradition, believers have been encouraged to practise severe penances, to discipline what were perceived to be endemic 'sins of the flesh'. The powerful ego was regarded as the enemy of spiritual life, an enemy upon which each person must mount a frontal assault in order to defeat one's sinfulness. But rather than this 'muscular' search for virtue we can remember that moral failure is often the result of egoic forces gone awry, of ego refusing to respond to the voice of soul operating as our conscience. We can learn to observe how and why ego makes spiritually dangerous moves. *We can develop spiritual practices which strengthen the work of soul.* We can learn to accept and love ourselves as periodically conflicted persons who are always held in the unconditional Loving of the Sacred Presence and by whose grace renewed life is always possible.

Think, for example, of the positive self-regard and self-respect which ego seeks to establish for the self. Personal humility - one of soul's most precious gifts - does not require a denial or suppression of these personal attributes carefully nurtured by ego. Humility comes as a gift of the Sacred through soul to teach us that *all our creative talents and virtues are to be welcomed and understood as gifts of the Sacred.* In this way we learn to resist a temptation to egoic self-congratulation and pride for our achievements and to discover gratitude for and celebration of creative ego work. Classical Christian theology understands this process very well and names it "grace completing nature".

A false and dangerous work of ego is to make us feel and believe that one or more of our many limited personae is our full true self. This is a situation of 'mistaken identity', a condition of 'living a lie'. Self-identification with one or more of our personae results in a foreshortening and dislocation of the process of becoming the full, rich personal mystery we are called to be. Soul work allows us to understand that each of our personae is only one expression of who we are, that the essential self is always a hidden mystery to be treasured and loved, always waiting to develop further.

One of the ongoing challenges of life is to identify and listen with respect and love to the creative urging within us. This teaches us that there is always new truth about ourselves waiting to be named, encouraged and realized. Each of us is a person rooted in the cosmic Mystery of the divine Loving, a person constantly being invited into new dimensions of who we are called to become. It is in this context that each person can discover the value of a careful practice of prayer for oneself.

Prayer for oneself frees the soul to be increasingly open to the interior, nurturing Sacred Presence. This work of soul needs to be strengthened if the misleading pretensions of egocentricity are to be successfully understood and challenged. Here is a beautiful, traditional prayer which seeks to open soul to the divine Light and Life:

> Come Thou, Love divine, seek Thou this soul of mine
> and visit it with thine own ardour glowing,
> Comforter draw near, within my heart appear
> and kindle it, thy holy Flame bestowing.
>
> Let it freely burn, 'til earthly passions
> turn to dust and ashes in its heat consuming.
> And let thy glorious light shine ever on my sight
> and clothe me 'round, my onward path illuming.
>
> Let holy charity my outward vesture be
> and lowliness my inner clothing,
> true lowliness of heart which takes the humbler part
> and o'er its own shortcoming weeps with loathing.
>
> And so the yearning strong
>   with which the soul will long
> shall far outpass the power of human telling,
> for none can tell its grace 'til one becomes the place
> wherein the Holy Spirit makes her dwelling.

This prayer is easily memorized, and can be said any time of day or night. And even greater depths in 'prayer for oneself' come from discovering one's own language to express deep spiritual desires, desires which seek the maturing of our spiritual life. For this work I constantly return for guidance to two useful admonitions:

> It is in the struggle to articulate truthfully that our words become actually capable of communicating truth. (Rosemary Haughton)

> Honest prayer begins with a willingness to be identified with the answer. (William Temple)

It has been said that "the head only knows what the heart knows, and what the heart knows today the head will understand tomorrow".

In the spiritual journey we listen to soul 'today' to be able to have understanding 'tomorrow'. Then we become able to challenge the false pretensions of ego. The more effectively we do this interior work, the more we enter into and are able to live our own truth.

THE CRUCIBLE OF PRAYER

Pilgrims of the spirit have always worked within a practice of personal and corporate prayer in order to discover the many paths of human spiritual expression and development. Within my own explorations in prayer at first I found that the solid words and firm edges of Christian tradition were helpful. But the more I traveled the pilgrim's Way the less useful they became in developing a creative practice of prayer. In fact solid words and firm edges blocked me. I needed new language within which to express my growing sense of the Divine, language by which to open myself to the Presence.

It takes months - sometimes years - of slow trial and error to shape prayer sufficiently fluid and open to enable our spiritual journey. Here is a text which gradually developed to become a mantra for me:

> Sacred Presence, Eternal Wisdom, Nurturing Spirit
> hidden from us in a Cloud of Unknowing
> known to us by interior awareness
> You surround us, You indwell us
> You call our hearts to a communion of love
> with Earth and all her creatures.
> In love You bind us to yourself
> revealing us to ourselves
> that our hearts may be tuned
> to the Music of the Universe
> to the Song of Creation.

This is not the language of univocal meaning. It is open and fluid, constantly inviting wide-ranging exploration by thoughts, feelings and aspirations. We need to go beyond Received Tradition to design personal prayer and public liturgies which stretch our minds and hearts in an adventure of faith for the 21st century. Our powers of desire, imagination, and perseverance are able to craft new language which facilitates the journey.

LOVING YEARNING GRIEVING

Embedded within the long record of Christian testimony to the Sacred Presence is frequent reference to a 'Divine Initiative'. We can recognize that personal faith is always a response to the Sacred, to the One Who constantly seeks an entry into our minds and hearts and deeds. One poet named this as an experience of "The Hound of Heaven". There is a wondrous doggedness in the divine Yearning as it seeks to win a willing response from the human heart. And in becoming aware of the divine Yearning we become able to recognize the genesis of our own human yearning to be open to the sacred dimensions of life. Personal prayer seeks to express this yearning.

At the heart of our awareness of the divine Yearning is a realization that we are loved without qualification. Sometimes this realization comes in response to an awareness that we don't 'deserve' to be loved. We recognize a Freedom and Generosity in the Sacred Presence that, once accepted, sustains us. Moreover, this is not a Loving which is cosy or unchallenging. This is a divine Passion which constantly summons and leads us into our own human becoming, into our own personal truth.

In the context of the divine Loving and Yearning we can become aware of the divine Grieving. This Grieving is a response to our willful refusals to accept the divine Loving; it is a response to our resistance to living with compassion and justice for others. More gentle than the ways of rebuke or judgment, divine Grieving may be sensed within the wounds of the body of the Crucified. Taken together, these three relationships - Loving, Yearning, Grieving - become a way of naming our experience of the Sacred Presence. This is a mythology of the Sacred inviting us to develop and articulate and live our own personal truth within the comprehensiveness of the Sacred.

To believe this is an invitation for us to learn, and daily to practice, creative loving, yearning and grieving in our relationships with other persons. By entering into these kinds of relationship we become more aware of the confusion and pain and creativity within people who are seeking meaning in life. We also learn to accept troubling aspects of our own lives and our need for spiritual healing.

> Sacred Presence, hidden and disclosed,
> You give yourself to us in overwhelming generosity.
> You break open our hearts with the floodtide of your Loving,
> You inflame our minds with the wonder of your Speaking.

You bind up our soul wounds with your gentle Compassion,
You gird our wills with the strength of your Spirit,
and you give us pilgrim friends with whom to share
the journey.
From dawn to dark, in joy and thanksgiving,
we celebrate your Presence in our lives,
our lives in your Presence.

PRAYER OF INTERCESSION

> To pray for another is to expose both oneself and him to the common ground of our being. It is to see one's concern for him in terms of ultimate concern [i.e. of the Sacred Presence]... Intercession is to be with another at that depth, whether in silence or compassion or action. It may consist simply in listening, when we take the otherness of the other person most seriously.
>
> (*Honest to God*, J.A.T. Robinson, p.99)

In this kind of prayer we hold a situation or person within our conscious, caring attention. We recall that the 'flowing energies of the divine Loving' are already present for them in compassion and healing. This is a way focusing our personal concern where the Divine Loving is already active. The work of intercession is never originated by us; it helps us to become more aware of and to participate in the needs of a particular situation or person. And sometimes intercession lead us to direct action.

Here is an example of responsible intercession, used by a community of Christian women in SE Asia:

Leader: Let us pray for the women in our community who just gave birth, but have no means to support their babies and families.

All: We so pray: grant us the courage to do something about it.

Leader: Let us pray for the women and men who have migrated to cities and abroad due to unemployment here.

All: We so pray: grant us the courage to do something about it.

Leader: Let us pray for the women who are physically and sexually abused within or outside the home.

All: We so pray: grant us the courage to do something about it.
[This is only a partial quote.]

The crucial element in this approach to intercession is the absence of any expectation of direct divine intervention, and a willingness of the intercessors to be enabled as a response to the need stated in the prayer.

Questions for discussion:

1. Name an example of your sense of self-worth as this relates to the creative role of ego.
2. Name characteristic ways in which you express 'soul' in relationships with other people.
3. Name one characteristic way in which you experience an inner 'contest' between ego and soul.
4. Describe characteristic ways in which you adapt successfully when present in an awkward social situation.
5. What personal qualities or goals seem important for your present spiritual growth?
6. How might you express in personal prayer your desire to receive these various gifts of the Spirit?

14

THE JOURNEY

I fled Him, down the nights and down the days;
I fled Him, down the arches of the years;
I fled Him, down the labyrinthine ways
Of my own mimd, and in the mist tears
I hid from him, and under running laughter.

> "The Hound of Heaven",
> Francis Thompson (1859-1907)

In the mid-1960s I participated in a ten-day workshop on personal development held in San Francisco. In the opening session the leader went around the circle of participants. Standing before each of us in turn he said, "My name is Ruel Howe. I am who I am, and I am still becoming. Will you help me with my becoming?" (*reply*: I will). He repeated this pattern as he stood before each group participant. It was a startling, memorable and effective beginning for our time together.

Each of us is able, by virtue of what we love and what we do well, to give something to the world that will show the fruit of our presence here. We are all called to add something to the creation of the universe. Each self is a work in progress; the result is the spiritual fashioning of a soul, and souls grow slowly.

Current evolutionary theory proposes that the cosmos expresses constant development. Everything is in a state of becoming or dying, nothing is static, everything is interconnected. A central spiritual quality built into each person is the potential to enter consciously into the evolution of her/his own self as a member of the whole. In this way we participate directly in the emerging life of the world. But this is not a 'straight-line' process: our interior development is a continuing, dynamic complex of interactions as part of one integrated process.

Each person is constantly involved in a functional interchange between thought and action, between the personal and the social, between matter and spirit, between the human and the Sacred. Each of us, with our personal needs and gifts, participates in personal development, in social relationships, and in Earth's material plenty. These multiple processes of personal life involve us constantly in *a creative process of challenge, adjustment and creative resolution.*

THE BIBLE AS ESSENTIAL RESOURCE

For nearly two centuries biblical scholars have been examining ancient manuscripts written in Hebrew or Greek (and a few in Aramaic and Coptic) to understand when, where, by whom, and for what reasons these documents were written. This process rigorously applies tools of historical, literary and archaeological analysis to explore why and how each text was written. Nevertheless, a resulting and enormous volume of literature about the Bible has not produced a unanimous verdict about 'what the Bible says'. There are many and various issues and points of view, both within the texts and about them. This sacred literature is not 'the Word of God'.

The continuing process of critical study has created three distinct groups of people. There are scholars dedicated to the process of detailed and expert study; there are careful students of this work who seek to absorb and use it in order to maximize their own understanding of the Bible; and there is an extensive group of readers/inquirers/believers who depend upon these students to relay basic information which can assist informed responses to the Bible. And even this very extensive work requires human imagination and intelligence as vital tools of understanding and action.

Readers of the Bible can learn to encounter the written words of the biblical text to receive a 'Living Word' of the Spirit. *It is this Living Word which seeks to engage us as people who are open to instruction, to continuing personal growth, and to compassionate actions of justice and peace.*

Biblical texts are a human and culturally-relative achievement. The Living Word is an interior and sacred Gift of Wisdom for personal formation and responsibility. Just as our experience of life is personal, fluid and unpredictable, so spiritual wisdom come with the same mysterious threefold characteristics.

There is no sense in which the Bible is "necessary for salvation". Indeed, for many people the notion of 'salvation' has been replaced by their search for 'transformation'. Biblical texts were originally brought into being by the Spirit and within a great many different human struggles. The result of that long and strenuous process was a collection of texts which have proved for many people to be food for the journey of life. These texts can be approached with a discriminating intelligence and an active imagination. In this way the Bible can help us to be open to the future precisely because it was written by people themselves caught up in an open-ended journey.

THAWING OUT THE BIBLICAL TEXT

Several years ago I participated in a one-day event led by the head of the Drama Department of a local university. The purpose of our time together was to help the participants improve how we read biblical texts in public liturgies. The leader pointed out how many biblical texts describe encounters between important actors and that in these texts human interactions had been 'frozen into words'. Our function as readers is to 'thaw out the words' so that the original situation might in some manner be experienced anew by the hearers.

This admonition applies equally to personal reading of the Bible. It suggests that whenever we read biblical texts we should use a sanctified imagination. *Texts appear to be inert words, but in fact they hold and intend to share past, lived experiences.* Our responsibility as readers is to attend carefully so that we become able to tease out the feelings, questions, sorrows, joys and insights which originally caused a particular event to be remembered and recorded. Over time this record becomes a source for our personal journey.

Here is a gospel text asking to be 'thawed out':

> Mark 8:24-30: Jesus got up and left that place and went off to the neighbourhood of Tyre. There he went into a house and wanted no one to know where he was. But it proved impossible to remain hidden. For no sooner had he got there, than a woman who had heard about him, and who had a daughter possessed by an evil spirit, arrived and prostrated herself before him. She was a Greek, a Syrophoenician by birth, and she asked him to drive the evil spirit out of her daughter. Jesus said to her, "You must let the children have all they want first. It is not right, you know, to take the children's food and throw it to the dogs." But she replied, "Yes, Lord, l know, but even the dogs under the table eat what the children leave." "If you can answer like that," Jesus said to her, "you can go home! The evil spirit has left your daughter." And she went back to her home and found the child lying quietly on her bed, and the evil spirit gone. (J.B. Phillips' translation)

As so often, Jesus is surrounded by a crowd who have heard about his fame as a teacher and healer. We can feel the pressure of many bodies upon one another. It was more than a little daring for this Gentile woman to push herself forward and speak to the Master when antagonism between Jew and Gentile was so much in the air. So it is not surprising that Jesus declined her first request, especially when we remember that he had left his own country for some respite from the immediate needs of his own people. What is surprising is her response to his refusal: she challenges him to reconsider - to realize that even Gentiles need his love and care.

The impact on Jesus of this woman's claim upon him is palpable. Had he not always believed that his mission was solely for his own people? And now to be challenged in this way by a Gentile woman! I wonder if he paused involuntarily, recognizing that to respond positively to her might forever alter how he understood his work. She was asking him to change his mind - just as we must sometimes change ours. To thaw out a text allows one's imagination to bring to life what was at the time of writing very lively indeed. There is much open space for us to occupy and explore as we reflect on biblical texts.

THE BOOK OF PSALMS

I am not a monastic; but I decided years ago to read psalms each day, together with some history of those ancient times. I soon realized that simple recitation taught me little; I decided to learn how *'to eavesdrop'* on the psalmists. This allowed me to tune into their hopes and fears and struggles. Here are the results of my eavesdropping on Psalm 40.

PSALM 40 - adapted from the Gelineau Psalter. In this 'journey psalm' we can feel the singer's struggle with the Holy One, with herself, and with her community of faith.

> I waited, I waited for Yahweh,
> again and again He stooped to me,
> He heard my longing cry.
> He drew me from the deadly pit, from the miry clay.

He set my feet upon a rock and made my footsteps firm.
He put a new song into my mouth, praise of our God;
many shall see and wonder and shall trust in Yahweh.
How many, Yahweh my God, are the wonders and designs
You have worked in Creation: You have no equal.
Should I proclaim and speak of them
they are more than I can tell.
Yet, You do not ask for sacrifice and offerings,
but an open heart.
You do not ask for sacred fire and victim;
instead, here am I.
In the scroll of the book it stands written
that I should do your will.
My God, I delight in your instruction;
in the depths of my heart I delight to do your will.
I have not hidden your justice in my heart
but have declared your faithful help.
I have not hidden your love and your truth
from the great assembly, my lips I have not sealed.
But I am beset with evils too many to be counted,
the follies of my people are without number,
we heap sin upon sin.
My own soul wounds conspire against me,
they are more than the hairs of my head,
and my heart sinks.
But you will not withhold your compassion from me.
Your love and your truth will always guard and guide me.
Though I am weak and poor, You know me.
You are my rescuer, my help: O God, do not delay.

This text brings to me many thoughts and feelings. The opening, "He heard my longing cry", gives me a sense of the yearning heart that drives the spiritual search of the singer. Her continuing struggle is daily rewarded. Her response is immense gratitude, including a new recognition that altar sacrifices cannot begin to be compared with the offering of an open heart and mind. However, her public sharing of renewed faith in Yahweh has not brought positive recognition nor response. Moreover, both she and her people constantly exhibit culpable foolishness and disobedience. But even so, she enters the future confident of divine companionship. Each time I enter this person's world I am encouraged to seek wisdom and courage for my own path.

Questions for discussion:

1. To what extent would you describe your experience of Christianity as 'a journey'?
2. What ways are open to you to strengthen your spiritual journey?
3. What present resources are available to you to deepen and continue and this journey?

15

CREATING A PILGRIM'S NOTEBOOK

For many centuries, three times each day a local church bell rang the Angelus, and people were reminded to pause and to recite the heart of their Christian faith. They stopped work and rehearsed basic values in their lives as they prayed the Pater Noster and the Ave Maria. By reciting this simple Christian mantra, the Sacred became present for them. And five times each day, in Islamic nations, millions of Muslims are called to prayer from a local minaret to renew their affection for and loyalty to the Prophet and his God. But in our highly secularized and frenetic Western industrial culture, if we desire to learn about the Christian Way, we must make a deliberate personal choice for a time and place to make this possible.

Daily exposure to selected parts of the Story of the Christian Tradition in the Bible is important for spiritual life. This regular practice is best supported if we create a personal 'Pilgrim's Notebook' in which to place thoughts which reveal and record our journey. The Notebook will also invite the practice and development of personal prayer. The language of prayer usually comes slowly as we are guided by head and heart. This important work is best done slowly and deliberately, seeking the guidance of the Spirit. Here are two of my prayers which developed over a few years.

Sacred Presence, timeless Wisdom, nurturing Spirit,
   hidden from us in a Cloud of Unknowing,
   revealed to us in moments of interior awareness,
You surround us, You indwell us,
You call us to a communion of love
   with Earth and all her creatures.
You bind us to yourself, tuning our hearts
   to the Music of the Universe
   to the Song of Creation,
In trust, gratitude and joy
   we open our hearts and minds to you,
Living Word, Light within, wondrous Generosity.

Sacred Presence, Ground of Being,
Wellspring of Truth and Loving,
   everywhere hidden, everywhere disclosed:
   in the unfolding patterns and powers of the Universe,
   in the beauty and rhythms of Nature,
   in each creature's struggle to fulfil its purpose,
   and as a wondrous quickening of the human spirit,
You are both hidden and disclosed.
But in gracious words and deeds of people
   in lives of prophets and sages
   and pre-eminently in Jesus of Nazareth
You are less hidden and more disclosed.

Robert C. Wild

MEDITATION based on the IGNATIAN METHOD

- Sit in a comfortable chair where you are unlikely to be disturbed.

- Using a New Testament, locate one scene in the gospels where Jesus is engaged with people.

- Begin meditation with prayer to the Spirit for guidance.

- Read the text over slowly, three times, conjuring up the scene in your imagination.

- Supply as many additional details as are consistent with the text.

- Find yourself in the scene.

- Notice Jesus, and how he is participating in the action.

- Listen to his words.

- Notice your responses to the entire scene.

- When you are finished, record anything which seems significant.

A dedicated and disciplined imagination can open us to a Living Word.

END NOTE ON DEPTH PSYCHOLOGY

Depth psychology "focuses on the psyche, human development, personality formation, and individuation. Individuation is a process of bringing our unconscious potential into a concrete living reality. This process helps to secure a bridge between an individual and the unconscious as well as the individual and his/her wider community. By incorporating both an inner and outer exploration, one discovers a more potent sense of meaning and purpose in life" (taken from the internet).

In his book "Insearch", James Hillman reports that "Depth psychologists – especially C.G. Jung – seemed to find soul and a living God image... [by] turning within, down to the 'ground of being'... the phenomenological place for the unconscious is down and in." (p. 49).

"The classical demonstrations of the unconscious are all of the 'stumbling' sort: forgetting and remembering, habit, slips of the tongue, word-association experiments, multiple personality, complexes (bundles of feeling toned ideas), mood and emotion, symptoms, dreams" (*ibid*, p.50 ff)

SELECT BIBLIOGRAPHY

Anderson, Bernhard W. "Out of the Depths", Westminster Press 1974

Armstrong, Karen. "The Great Transformation", A. Knoff, 2006

Berry, Thomas, & Swimme, Brian. "The Universe Story", Harper Collins, 1994

Bonhoeffer, D. "Letters and Papers from Prison", Fontana Books. 1964

Borg, Marcus. "Evolution of the Word", Harper One. 2012

Brueggemann, W. "The Prophetic Imagination", Fortress Press. 2001

Bringhurst, R. "Everywhere Being is Dancing", Gaspereau Press. 2007

Chesterton, G.K. "Francis of Assisi", Hodder & Stoughton. 1960

Cobb, J. "Process Theology", R. Mesle, ed., Chalice Press, 1993

Eiseley, L. "The Firmament of Time", Atheneum. 1971

Fiorenza, Elisabeth S. "Wisdom Ways: Feminist Biblical Interpretation". Orbis Books, 2001

Finklestein & Silberman "The Bible Unearthed", Simon & Schuster. 2002

Griffin, D. R. (ed) "Spirituality and Society", Univ. of New York Press. 1988

Griffin, D.R. (ed) "The Reenchantment of Science", Univ. of New York Press, 1988

Hertzog, W.R. "Parables as Subversive Speech", Westminster Press. 1994

Hillman, James "Insearch". Charles Scribner, 1967

Horsley & Hanson, "Bandits, Prophets and Messiahs", Harper SanFrancisco. 1985

Malone, Mary. T. "Women and Christianity", Orbis Books, 2003.

Mannheim, K. "Ideology and Utopia", Harcort, Brace, & World. 1936

McTaggart, L. "The Field", HarperCollins. 2002

Meier, J.P. "A Marginal Jew": Vol 2, Doubleday Anchor. 1994

Ricoeur, P. "The Symbolism of Evil", Beacon Press. 1967

Ross, R. "Returning to the Teachings", Penguin Books, 1996

Tawney, R.H. Tawney, R.H. "Religion and the Rise of Capitalism", Harcourt, Brace & Co. 1926

Teilhard de Chardin, P. "The Phenomenon of Man", Harper Torchbook. 1961

_____ "Le Milieu Divin", Fontana Books. 1965

Theisson, Gerd. "Social Reality and the Early Christians", Fortress Press, 1992

Underhill, E. "The Golden Sequence", Harper Torchbook. 1960

The New Oxford Annotated Bible (NRSV), Oxford University Press, 1991

ABOUT BOB WILD

Born in 1927, Robert Wild grew up in Montreal, Québec and graduated BA '49 from McGill University. He did post-graduate studies in theology in Saskatoon, Vancouver and Toronto, and served in the Anglican Church of Canada for 36 years. Most of his career he served in parishes in southern Ontario, Vancouver and Edmonton. He also worked as a supply priest for small rural parishes in Saskatchewan and as a Chaplain at the University of Saskatchewan.

Throughout his working life Bob has been interested in the mystics and in biblical scholarship. Always he adopted a questioning attitude to mainstream church doctrines. He has led many study groups and retreats during his lifetime, constantly encouraging participants to be critically discerning.

Bob is the author of three books in addition to A Primer for Spirituality in the 21st Century: Frontiers of the Spirit (1981), Sacred Presence – in Search of the New Story (2004), and Sacred Journey (2006). He is always interested to engage with his readers and can be contacted by email at wildacre.2@shaw.ca

CPSIA information can be obtained
at www.ICGtesting.com
Printed in the USA
LVHW041027150819
627694LV00002B/2/P

9 780228 816065